What Will I Do With
All Those Zucchini?

Elaine Borish, an American living in London, was born in New York City. She holds degrees from Rutgers, Boston University, and Northeastern University and has taught at universities in New England. In old England, she has lectured in English and American literature at Morley College in London. Her numerous articles have appeared in leading newspapers and magazines.

Also by Elaine Borish

A Legacy of Names
Literary Lodgings
Novel Cuisine
This Book Is Unpublishable!
What Will I Do With All Those Courgettes?

Elaine Borish

What Will I Do With All Those Zucchini?

Fidelio Press

Telluride · London

Dedicated to the avid gardener who keeps me supplied with copious courgettes and a zillion zucchini

Published by
Fidelio Press, Inc.
129 Aldasoro Road
Telluride CO 81435

ISBN 0-9524881-6-7
ISBN 978-0-9524881-6-3

Library of Congress Control Number: 2005910670

Printed in the United States

Cover design by Kate Chitham

"What Will I Do With All Those" is a trademark of Fidelio Press, Inc.

PREFACE

Courgettes or zucchini mean exactly the same thing. And marrows are simply overgrown zucchini. Whether you call them courgettes (as the English and French do) or zucchini (as do Americans and Italians), gardens can yield enormous amounts, especially for people involved in growing their own organic food. This book was inspired by two stories:

I asked Larry what he does with the vast quantities of the zucchini crop I had just seen him harvest. "Well," he replied unblinking, "I put them in a large brown paper bag, go to a neighbor's house and place them on the doorstep. Then I ring the doorbell—and run like hell!"

Kathy, an avid gardener who grows a wide variety of vegetables in her extensive garden, recalls her growing-up days in Iowa when one did not dare to leave the car door unlocked in the summertime. Anyone who failed to use a key took the risk of returning to find the car filled with zucchini.

The great thing about an abundant crop is the infinite variety of ways in which to use it. No need to rack your brain for ideas for cooking them. Here are some one hundred fifty easy-to-prepare and good recipes for consuming the entire crop. They must be easy because I've made them—and good because Marty helps me eat them.

Even if you do not have a garden, you can grow zucchini at home in a tub on the balcony or in some outdoor space. Freshly picked when they are still small, zucchini are remarkably good. Be warned, you may develop a passion for this wonderful and versatile vegetable.

And remember, my favorite word in giving recipes is "about" because preparation should be easy and fun, and undue concern for exactness should not outweigh your own logical application.

Courgette

Zucchini

CONTENTS

PREFACE

SOUPS

Favorite Zucchini Soup	2
Zucchini Potato Soup	3
Zucchini and Mint Soup	4
Zucchini Soup with Mint	5
Zucchini Watercress Soup	6
Zucchini and Dill Soup	7
Tomato-Zucchini Soup	8
Zucchini and Fennel Soup	9
Zucchini Pesto Soup	10
Curry Zucchini Soup	12
Sliced Zucchini Soup	13
Ratatouille Soup	14
Minestrone	15
Spring Vegetable Soup	16
Thai Soup with Cellophane Noodles	17
Zucchini Bisque	18
Gazpacho	19
Mexican Zucchini Blossom Soup	20

SALADS

Chunky Salad with Zucchini	22
Zucchini and Radicchio Salad	23
Raw Zucchini Salad in Radicchio Cups	24
Raw Zucchini and Mushroom Salad	25
Raw Zucchini Julienne Salad	26
Zucchini and Chives Salad	27
Mashed Zucchini Salad	28
Marinated Zucchini	29
Zucchini Vinaigrette	30
Pasta Salad Sweet and Sour	31
Rice Salad with Zucchini and Peppers	32
Layered Vegetable Salad	33
Pickled Zucchini	34
Zucchini Chutney	35

APPETIZERS

Cruditiés with Vinaigrette	38
Zucchini Appetizer Salad	39
Carpaccio Zucchini	40
Zucchini Paté	41
Ratatouille	43
Zucchini à la Grecque	44
Zucchini Fritters	45
Fried Zucchini Appetizer	46
Zucchini and Mushrooms in Soy Sauce	47
Zucchini Parmesan	48
Marinated Zucchini and Eggplant	49
Zucchini Timbales	50
Mediterranean Vegetables with Tahini	51
Hummus with Zucchini	52
Zucchini Bruschetta	53
Fried Stuffed Zucchini Flowers	54
Italian Zucchini Flowers	55
Baked Stuffed Zucchini Flowers	56

LUNCH or SUPPER

Pisto	58
Zucchini Omelet	59
Zucchini Pancake	60
Zucchini-Carrot Kugel	61
Zucchini-Carrot Latkes	62
Frittata of Zucchini	63
Zucchini Soufflé	64
Vegetable Quiche	65
Zucchini Pudding	66
Vegetable Kebabs	67
Stuffed Pasta Shells	68
Zucchini Boats	69
Zucchini Ripiene	70
Mediterranean Zucchini Bake	71
Risotto with Spring Vegetables	73
Spicy African Stew	75
Pitta with Zucchini and Carrots	76
Pizza with Zucchini	77
Ciabatta Rolls with Zucchini and Tomato-Saffron Sauce	79

CASSEROLES

Zucchini Casserole	82
Marrow Casserole	83
Zucchini Cheese Casserole	84
Zucchini Parmesan Casserole	85
California Zucchini Cheese Casserole	86
Spicy Zucchini and Potato Mash	87
Zucchini Custard Casserole	88
Summer Zucchini and Mushroom Bake	89
Winter Stew	90
Zucchini Orange Bake	91
Vegetable Macaroni Bake	92
Zucchini-Spaghetti Casserole	93
Zucchini and Potato Casserole	94
Italian Vegetable Casserole	95
Zucchini and Eggplant Crumble	96
Baked Zucchini Casserole	97
Mashed Zucchini Casserole	98
Zucchini Couscous	99
Vegetable Bourguignonne	100

MAIN COURSES

Neapolitan Zucchini and Eggplant with Pasta	102
Lasagna with Zucchini	103
Zucchini Sausage Bake	104
Zucchini Tian	105
Rustic Vegetable Stew	106
Chili Sin Carne	107
Gado-Gado	108
Fish in Foil	110
Indian Prawns with Zucchini	111
Lamb Biryani	112
Imam Bayildi	113
Mediterranean Chicken with Zucchini	114
Veal Cutlets with Zucchini	115
Chinese Ground Beef with Zucchini and Tomatoes	116

ACCOMPANIMENTS

Basic Zucchini with Fresh Herbs	118
Sautéed Zucchini in Olive Oil	119
Sautéed Zucchini with Herbs	120
Sautéed Zucchini with Yogurt	121
Turkish Zucchini with Yogurt	122
Zucchini with Tomatoes and Garlic	123
Stuffed Zucchini	124
Zucchini with Chick Pea Stuffing	125
Zucchini with Parmesan Cheese	126
Zucchini with Apricots	127
Sweet and Sour Zucchini	128
Sicilian Style Sweet and Sour Zucchini	129
Zucchini Strips with Mint	130
Zucchini and Carrots à la Menthe	131
Dijon Carrots and Zucchini	132
Poor Person's Zucchini	133
Lemon Zucchini	134
Zucchini with Oil and Lemon	135
Grated Zucchini with Lemon Juice	136
Zucchini à l'orange	137
Zucchini Fans	138
Marrow in Tomato and Coriander Sauce	139
Spicy Ginger Marrow	140
Mexican Zucchini and Corn in Tomato Sauce	141
Puebla Style Zucchini	142
Zucchini Rice	143
Farfalle with Zucchini, Peas, and Mint	144
Baked Zucchini with Goat Cheese	145
Zucchini and Cheese Gratin	146
Grilled Garlic Zucchini	147
Baked Zucchini Sticks	148
Baked Zucchini with Tomatoes	149
Roasted Summer Vegetables	150
Cheese-Stuffed Zucchini	151
Vermouth Zucchini with Onions	152
Curried Zucchini	153
Southwestern Zucchini with Corn and Green Chiles	154

BREAD and CAKE

Zucchini Bread	156
Zucchini Spice Bread	157
Zucchini Pineapple Bread	158
Zucchini Muffins	159
Carrot and Zucchini Cake	160
Wholemeal Zucchini and Raisin Cake	161
Chocolate Zucchini Layer Cake	162
Chocolate Zucchini Cake	164
Zucchini Bread Loaf	165

RANDOM RECIPES FOR ROTUND MARROWS

Marrow Ginger Jam	168
Stuffed Marrow Rings	169
And more marrows….	170

TABLE OF WEIGHTS AND MEASURES   171

COMMENTS ON ZUCCHINI   172

Soups

Favorite Zucchini Soup

The first zucchini soup I ever made, equally good hot or cold, remains a favorite because it is easy to make as well as delicious—and the ingredients keep guests guessing. Make double or triple quantities, as this soup freezes well.

3 medium zucchini (about 1 lb or 450 g), cut into thick slices
24 fl oz (3 cups or 700 ml) chicken stock
1 medium onion, sliced
¼ teaspoon oregano
¼ teaspoon rosemary
salt and pepper, to taste

1. Place all the ingredients into a large pot and bring to a boil. Reduce heat, cover and simmer for about 15-20 minutes.
2. Blend in a food processor until smooth. Add more water if necessary. Reheat when ready to serve. Or chill and serve cold.

6 servings

Zucchini Potato Soup

Serve hot in winter or chilled in summer.

2 medium potatoes, peeled and sliced
2 cans chicken broth (about 28 fl oz or 800 ml)
2 medium zucchini, sliced
3-4 spring onions, sliced
1 medium onion, sliced
2 tablespoons butter
salt and pepper to taste
2 teaspoons thyme, or to taste

1. Cook potatoes in chicken broth until almost tender. Add sliced zucchini and cook until soft.
2. Sauté spring onions and onions in butter over low heat until transparent.
3. Add salt and pepper and thyme. Purée all ingredients in a food processor until smooth.
4. Serve with a dollop of yogurt or sour cream.

Serves 6-8

Zucchini and Mint Soup

Here's another soup that may be served either hot or cold.

2 oz (50 g) butter
2 medium onions, chopped
2 lbs (900 g) zucchini, cut into chunks
24 oz (3 cups or 700 ml) chicken stock
2 handfuls of mint leaves
salt
freshly ground black pepper

1. In a large pot, melt the butter and add the chopped onions. Sauté over low heat until the onions are soft and translucent, about 10 minutes. Add the zucchini and cook for an additional 5 minutes.
2. Add the chicken stock and 1 handful of mint leaves.
3. Cover and simmer for 30 minutes. Cool.
4. Blend the contents in a food processor together with the remaining handful of mint leaves.
5. Add more water if needed and season with salt and pepper.

Serves 6

Zucchini Soup with Mint

*Similar to the previous recipe, this zucchini-and-mint soup
variation includes potato and yields a thick texture and
delectable flavor.*

2 oz (50 g) butter
1 bunch of spring onions
1 garlic clove, finely
  chopped
1 medium potato, cut into
  cubes
salt and pepper
2 large zucchinis, grated

24 fl oz (3 cups or 700 ml)
  chicken or vegetable
  stock
7 fl oz (200 ml) milk
handful of mint leaves
handful of flat leaf parsley
Parmesan cheese

1. Melt the butter in a pot and add sliced spring onions and chopped garlic. Cook and stir for about five minutes, until soft but not brown.
2. Add the potato cubes and cook for a few minutes more. Add salt and pepper to taste.
3. Add the grated zucchinis and continue cooking for another few minutes.
4. Add stock and simmer for five minutes, or until potato is tender.
5. Add milk, mint, and parsley. Bring to a boil. Then blend in a food processor.
6. Return to pot and reheat. Adjust seasonings and serve with grated Parmesan cheese.

Serves 6

Zucchini Watercress Soup

Here's another delicious variation that makes a perfect beginner to almost any dinner.

4 tablespoons butter
2 medium onions, chopped
24 fl oz (3 cups or 700 ml) chicken stock
5-6 medium zucchini (2 lbs or nearly 1 kg), cut into small pieces
1 large bunch watercress (about 4 loosely-packed cups or 100 g)
3 tablespoons fresh lemon juice
salt and pepper, to taste

1. Melt butter, add onions, and cook in a large covered pot over low heat until onions are soft and golden (about 15-20 minutes).
2. Add chicken stock and bring to a boil. Add zucchini and simmer, covered, until zucchini are tender (about 20 minutes).
3. Add watercress. Remove pot from heat, cover, and allow to stand for 5 minutes.
4. Purée soup in food processor until smooth.
5. Return to pot and add lemon juice. Season with salt and pepper.
6. Add additional stock, if necessary, to obtain desired consistency. Heat when ready to serve.

Serves 6

Zucchini and Dill Soup

You may want to add more stock (up to another pint) for a thinner consistency, but be cautious with the amount of dill as it is a strong herb.

1 medium onion, chopped
2 oz (50 g) butter
1 large zucchini, peeled and sliced
2 teaspoons flour
35 fl oz (4¼ cups or 1 litre) stock
salt and pepper to taste
2 egg yolks
2 tablespoons heavy cream
extra pat of butter
dill weed

1. Sauté the onion in butter in a large pot for 5 minutes. Add the sliced zucchini, cover and cook for another 5 minutes, until vegetables are golden.
2. Sprinkle in the flour and stir. Add about half the liquid and simmer until zucchini slices are just cooked.
3. Purée in a blender or food processor. Return to pot and add the remaining stock and the salt and pepper. Reheat.
4. In a bowl, beat together the egg yolks and cream and pour a ladleful of the soup into the egg mixture. Blend it all together and pour the mixture back into the pot. Stir over a low heat just to bind the soup smoothly.
5. Add the pat of butter. Sprinkle with chopped dill weed and serve.

Serves 6-8

Tomato-Zucchini Soup

Another soup that is good either hot or cold.

2 tablespoons olive oil
2 medium onions, sliced
5-6 small zucchini, sliced
35 fl oz (4¼ cups or 1 litre) chicken broth
2 large tomatoes, skinned and chopped
1 small bunch parsley, finely chopped
1 tablespoon chopped chives
1 teaspoon salt
pinch of sugar
4-5 chopped fresh basil leaves or ½ teaspoon dried basil
2 teaspoons lemon juice

1. In a large pot, heat the oil and add the onion and zucchini. Cover and cook slowly for 10 minutes.
2. Add the chicken broth and simmer for an additional 20 minutes.
3. Remove zucchini and onions from broth and purée together with tomatoes in a blender or food processor. Return the zucchini mixture to pot and add the rest of the ingredients. Cook 5 minutes more. Serve hot or cold.

Serves 8

Zucchini and Fennel Soup

The fennel imparts a mild and refreshing aniseed flavor to this soup, which you can make ahead of time and reheat when needed.

3 oz (80 g) butter
1 large onion, chopped
1 lb (450 g) zucchini, sliced
1 lb (450 g) leaves of fennel bulb, cut into small pieces
5 fl oz (150 ml) dry sherry
½ teaspoon salt
freshly ground black pepper
½ teaspoon sugar
32-35 fl oz (4-4¼ cups or 900 ml-1 litre) stock

1. Melt the butter in a pot and add chopped onions. Sauté slowly until golden.
2. Add zucchini and fennel together with sherry, salt and pepper, and sugar.
3. Pour in stock. Cover and simmer on low heat for 40-45 minutes.
4. Liquidize in a food processor.
5. Adjust seasonings and add more water or stock as needed.
6. Reheat just before serving.

Serves 8-10

Zucchini Pesto Soup

This soup is good in the summertime, served warm rather than hot, together with good, fresh bread.

3 tablespoons olive oil
2 medium onions, chopped
4 small zucchini (about 1½ lbs or 700 g) cut in ½-inch
   (1.2 cm) cubes
3 medium potatoes, peeled and cut in 1-inch (2.5 cm) cubes
16 fl oz (2 cups or 450 ml) chicken stock
32 fl oz (4 cups or 900 ml) water
2 oz (50 g) spaghetti broken into 1-inch (2.5 cm) pieces
salt and pepper to taste
3 large cloves garlic, chopped
2 handfuls basil leaves
1 handful parsley leaves
1 tablespoon pine nuts (optional)
2 oz (50 g) grated Parmesan cheese
2-3 tablespoons olive oil

1. Heat the 3 tablespoons olive oil in a large pot over medium heat. Add onions and cook for about 15 minutes until golden. Add the zucchini and potatoes and cook, continuing to stir occasionally, for another 10 minutes.
2. Add the stock and water. Increase the heat to medium-high to reach boiling point. Then reduce heat and simmer, uncovered, for 30 minutes.
3. Add the spaghetti and the salt and pepper. Simmer about 10 minutes, until the spaghetti is cooked.

4. Blend the garlic, basil and parsley (and pine nuts, if used) in a food processor. Add the cheese and blend it in. While processing, slowly stream in the olive oil until the mixture forms a thick paste. Add salt and pepper to taste. Turn the pesto out into a large bowl.

5. Ladle about 1 cup of the soup into the pesto and combine, stirring briskly. Return this mixture to the soup remaining in the pot and mix it all together. Remove from the heat, cover, and allow to stand for 5 minutes. Adjust seasonings.

6. Sprinkle additional cheese into each bowl of soup and serve.

6-8 servings

Curry Zucchini Soup

This is another soup that may be eaten hot or cold, winter or summer—and freezes well.

3 or 4 medium zucchini, sliced
1 medium onion, chopped
2 oz (¼ cup or 50 g) rice
20 oz (2½ cups or 600 ml) chicken stock
1 teaspoon salt
1 teaspoon curry powder
1 teaspoon mustard
4-8 oz (½-1 cup or 100-225 g) yogurt

1. Place zucchini, onion, rice, chicken stock, and salt in a large pot.
2. Add water, if necessary, to cover zucchini and simmer until zucchini are tender, about 15 minutes.
3. Blend in a food processor together with curry powder, mustard, and yogurt.

Serves 8

Sliced Zucchini Soup

Here is another way to use zucchini—with a crunch—in soup.

1 large onion, chopped
celery stalk, chopped
2 tablespoons olive oil
8 oz (1 cup or 225 g) raw rice
4 tomatoes, peeled, seeded, and chopped
48 fl oz (6 cups or approximately 1.4 litres) chicken or beef
  broth
4 small zucchini
5 tablespoons minced fresh chives or parsley
salt and freshly ground black pepper
grated Parmesan cheese

1. Sauté coarsely-chopped onion and celery in olive oil until onions turn golden.
2. Add rice and cook another 3 minutes, stirring frequently.
3. Add tomatoes and broth. Cook over medium heat until rice is just tender.
4. Add thinly-sliced zucchini and the chives or parsley and cook covered for about 5 minutes. (Add more water, if needed.) The zucchini should still be crisp. Season with salt and pepper to taste.
5. Serve hot with grated Parmesan cheese on the side.

Serves 8-10

Ratatouille Soup

A hearty soup that is thick and textured.

1 ½ tablespoons olive oil
1 large onion, chopped
1 green pepper, chopped
2 cloves garlic, chopped
1 ½ lbs (700 g) eggplant, peeled and cut into ¼-inch (.6 cm) cubes
2 1-lb (450 g) tins tomatoes, undrained, chopped
3-4 medium-large zucchini, unpeeled
32 fl oz (4 cups or 900 ml) water or stock (vegetable or chicken)
1 bay leaf
1 ¼ teaspoons dried basil
1 ¼ teaspoons dried oregano
salt and pepper to taste
6 oz (175 g) of any very small pasta

1. Heat oil in a large soup pot. Add onions, green pepper, and garlic. Cook about 5 minutes, until tender.
2. Add cubed eggplant. Cook 5 minutes, stirring frequently and adding water if necessary to prevent sticking.
3. Add tomatoes together with zucchini that has been cut in half lengthwise, then into ¼-inch (.6 cm) slices. Add water or stock and spices. Bring to a boil, then reduce to low heat, and cover and cook for 45 minutes.
4. Add pasta, cover and cook for 10 minutes.
5. Discard bay leaf and serve.

8 servings

Minestrone

The beans, pasta, and chunky vegetables can make this hearty
soup a meal when served with hot crusty bread.

8 oz (225 g) dried haricot beans
2 tablespoons olive oil
1 medium onion, chopped
3-4 cloves garlic, minced
1 stalk celery, finely chopped
1 large carrot, diced
1 small can tomatoes
34 fl oz (about 4¼ cups or 1 litre) vegetable stock
4 oz (100 g) small fine pasta such as conchigliette
1 zucchini, cubed or thinly sliced
salt and freshly ground pepper
4 tablespoons finely chopped parsley
2 oz (50 g) grated Parmesan cheese

1. Soak the beans in cold water overnight. On the following day, drain and put them in a saucepan, covering them with fresh water. Simmer until nearly tender, about 20 minutes.
2. Heat the olive oil in a pot and add the onion, garlic, celery and carrot. Cover pot and simmer for about 10 minutes, stirring occasionally. Add the tomatoes (broken up) and stock. Cover and simmer for 1 hour.
3. Mix in the beans and add the pasta and zucchini. Add salt to taste and grind in some pepper. Add more boiling stock if needed. Cook until pasta is tender. Sprinkle with parsley and Parmesan cheese and serve.

Serves 8-10

Spring Vegetable Soup

Here is another flavorful and colorful soup to add to your easy weekday repertory. Serve with ciabatta or other rustic bread.

2 tablespoons olive oil
1 small onion, finely chopped
2 garlic cloves, finely chopped
1 medium potato, diced
20 fl oz (2½ cups or 600 ml) vegetable or chicken stock
1 carrot, sliced diagonally (or turnip)
4 oz (110 g) curly kale (or spring greens)
2 oz (50 g) fresh or frozen peas
2 small zucchini, sliced
salt and pepper
chili oil (optional)
fresh flat-leaf parsley, coarsely chopped

1. Heat oil in a large pot and cook the onion, garlic and potato in it for 3-4 minutes, stirring occasionally, until softened.
2. Add stock and simmer for 5 minutes. Add carrots and continue cooking for 3 minutes. Then add kale, peas, and zucchini. Season and cook for another 2-3 minutes.
3. For a spicy flavor, add a few drops of chili oil. Serve, garnished with parsley.

Serves 4

Thai Soup with Cellophane Noodles

This easy-to-prepare soup will be even easier if you are able to buy small bundles of cellophane or rice noodles, rather than trying to cut some off from a big bundle.

**small bundle cellophane or mung bean noodles (or rice
    noodles), about 2 oz (50 g)
40 fl oz (5 cups or 1200 ml) chicken or vegetable stock
1 medium-large onion, thinly sliced
2-3 cloves garlic, minced
4-6 mushrooms, thinly sliced
2 small zucchini, thinly sliced
1 tablespoon soy sauce
salt and pepper**

1. Soak noodles in hot water until softened, and then cut them into short lengths.
2. Bring stock to a boil and add onion, garlic, and the drained and cut noodles. Cook until noodles are swollen and soft, about 10 minutes.
3. Add the mushrooms, zucchini, and soy sauce and cook until just tender but still crunchy, about 5 minutes. Add salt and pepper to taste and serve hot right away.

Serves 8-10

Zucchini Bisque

I relented on the cholesterol count for this recipe, which is made with butter and cream. (But skimmed milk may be substituted for the cream.)

1 medium onion, chopped
4 oz (100 g) butter
4-5 zucchini (about 1½ lbs or 700 g), shredded
24 fl oz (3 cups or 700 ml) chicken stock
1 teaspoon dried basil
½ teaspoon nutmeg
1 teaspoon salt
freshly ground black pepper
8 fl oz (1 cup or 240 ml) heavy cream

1. Melt butter in large pot and add chopped onion. Sauté until soft and golden.
2. Add shredded zucchini and chicken stock to the onion.
3. Cover pot and simmer for 15 minutes.
4. Purée contents, adding basil, nutmeg, salt and pepper.
5. Add cream and mix well. Serve hot or cold.

6-7 servings

Gazpacho

There are many variations of this refreshing summertime soup that comes from Spain. Why not add a raw cubed zucchini to vary this traditional cold soup?

3 large tomatoes, peeled
1 clove garlic
1 medium onion, sliced
1 green pepper, seeded
l cucumber, sliced (or half of a large one)
1 stalk celery
salt
½ teaspoon black pepper
5 tablespoons red wine vinegar
4 tablespoons olive oil
32 oz (4 cups or 900 ml) tomato juice

Garnish:
8 oz (225 g) bread cubes or croutons
1 onion, chopped
1 green pepper, chopped
1 zucchini, peeled and cubed

1. Purée tomatoes, garlic, onion, pepper, cucumber and celery in a food processor. Combine all ingredients in a large bowl, adding salt and pepper, wine vinegar, olive oil and tomato juice.
2. Chill overnight and serve ice cold.
3. Just before serving, add any or all garnish ingredients—bread cubes, onion, green pepper, and zucchini—or serve garnish ingredients separately for diners to help themselves.

Serves 8

Mexican Zucchini Blossom Soup

Save blossoms from your zucchini plants and store them in freezer until you accumulate enough to make this unusual, conversation-producing soup. For a dinner party, you may need to double this recipe, but the effort will undoubtedly double the party conversation, as you discuss the exotic secret ingredient. Note that since each flower weighs about ½ oz or 10 grams, you will need about 16 to 20 flowers.

32 fl oz (4 cups or 900 ml) chicken stock
4 oz (100 g) corn kernels, fresh or frozen
1 oz (25 g) butter
½ onion, finely chopped
1 clove garlic, crushed
1 tablespoon tomato purée
1 tablespoon chopped fresh coriander
2 oz (50 g) mushrooms, (about 6 medium-large mushrooms), sliced
8 oz (225 g) zucchini blossoms
freshly ground pepper to taste
2 tablespoons shredded cheese

1. Put the stock in a saucepan and bring to a boil. Add the corn and cook for 5 minutes.
2. Heat the butter in a frying pan and sauté the onion and garlic until limp. Add tomato purée, coriander, mushrooms and broken-up blossoms and sauté for a further 5 minutes. Sprinkle in a few grinds of pepper.
3. Add this mixture to the stock and serve hot, garnished with shredded cheese.

Serves 6

Salads

Chunky Salad with Zucchini

This is easy to prepare because everything—the amounts are not very crucial—is just mixed together to make a colorful salad. Other raw vegetables (such as broccoli or cauliflower) may be added.

1 small onion, chopped
½ green pepper, chopped
½ sweet red pepper, chopped
3-4 tomatoes, chopped
20 small stuffed green olives, sliced
20 small pitted black olives, sliced
8-10 mushrooms, sliced
1 carrot, thinly sliced
1 zucchini (8 oz or 225 g), unpeeled and cut into chunks
1 yellow zucchini or squash (8 oz or 225 g), cut into chunks
1 small cucumber or half a large one (8 oz or 225 g), cut in half lengthwise, then thinly sliced
2 tablespoons dried parsley flakes
½ teaspoon dried dill weed
¼ teaspoon garlic powder
2-3 fl oz (about ¼ cup or 75 ml) Italian dressing

1. Combine all ingredients in a large bowl and mix well.
2. Cover and chill, mixing several times before it is ready to be used.

Serves 8

Zucchini and Radicchio Salad

Use any good vinaigrette dressing, or the recipe below.

6 tablespoons vinaigrette dressing
1 clove garlic, minced
1 medium zucchini, thinly sliced
1 head radicchio
12-16 small pitted black olives
1 tablespoon pine nuts (pignoli)
salt and freshly ground black pepper

1. Place vinaigrette, garlic, and sliced zucchini in a salad bowl and toss. Allow to stand for a half hour for zucchini to absorb the flavor of the dressing.
2. Cut radicchio leaves into pieces and add to salad bowl together with black olives and pine nuts.
3. Season with salt and pepper. Toss with dressing before serving.

Serves 4-6

Dressing:
1 teaspoon French mustard
5 fl oz (150 ml) oil
4 tablespoons wine vinegar
salt and freshly ground black pepper
sugar to taste

1. Combine all ingredients in a small jar and cover tightly.
2. Mix well by shaking the jar, thoroughly blending together the ingredients.

Raw Zucchini Salad in Radicchio Cups

If radicchio is unavailable, substitute a red leaf lettuce such as frilly-edged Lollo Rosso to make an attractive-looking salad.

1 large zucchini, grated
1 carrot, grated
2-3 tablespoons French dressing
4 large radicchio leaves

1. Toss grated zucchini and grated carrots in a good, herbed French dressing.
2. Chill and serve in radicchio cups.

Serves 4

Raw Zucchini and Mushroom Salad

Requires no cooking—perfect on a hot summer day.

1 large zucchini, about 9 oz (250 g), sliced
6 oz (175 g) firm white mushrooms, sliced

Dressing:
4 tablespoons sunflower oil
2 tablespoons walnut or hazelnut oil
3 tablespoons lemon juice
¼ teaspoon pepper
1 teaspoon honey
1 clove garlic, crushed
1 tablespoon finely chopped spring onions or chives
2 tablespoons freshly chopped parsley

1. Place the sliced zucchini in a salad bowl together with the sliced mushrooms.
2. Whisk together all the dressing ingredients.
3. Toss gently and serve.

Serves 4-6

Raw Zucchini Julienne Salad

Substitute fresh basil, if you have it, to make the salad even more delicious.

4 small zucchini
1 spring onion, finely chopped
4-5 tablespoons olive oil
6 tablespoons red wine vinegar
½ teaspoon oregano
½ teaspoon basil
salt and pepper

Optional extras:
clove of garlic, crushed
red onion, minced
finely chopped parsley
thinly sliced mushrooms

1. Cut small zucchini into thin lengthwise slices, then cut thinly across the width to make julienne strips. Place in a bowl.
2. Add all other ingredients, mix gently, and chill in refrigerator until cold.

Serves 4

26

Zucchini and Chive Salad

If chives are unavailable, finely-cut spring onions may be substituted.

3 small zucchini (about 12 oz or 350 g)
1 tablespoon olive oil
juice of half a lemon
salt and freshly ground black pepper
2 tablespoons chopped chives

1. Place the zucchini in a large pan of boiling water for about 3 minutes, just long enough to reduce the bitterness of the skin. Drain immediately in a colander and rinse in cold water to stop them cooking.
2. Cut zucchini into slices ½-inch (1.2 cm) thick and place them in a shallow serving dish.
3. Blend the oil, lemon juice, salt and pepper, and pour this dressing over the zucchini.
4. Add the chopped chives and mix thoroughly. Refrigerate to chill the salad before serving.

Serves 4

Mashed Zucchini Salad

*Smaller zucchini, which do not have large seeds, will make a
smoother mash for this exotic salad.*

6-8 small zucchini (about 1 ½ lbs or 700 g)
juice of half a lemon
2 tablespoons olive oil
3 garlic cloves, crushed
1 teaspoon ground coriander
dash of pepper
salt to taste
10 black olives, cut into halves

1. Boil zucchini until they are soft. Drain and press out excess
   water. Cut up with a knife and then mash.
2. Add the other ingredients and mix all together. Serve cold.

Serves 6

Marinated Zucchini

This salad makes a good appetizer or a main course accompaniment. It may also be kept in the refrigerator for a week and used to enliven other salads or sandwiches.

3 small zucchini (about 1 lb or 450 g)
2 tablespoons olive oil
4 garlic cloves, crushed
salt and freshly ground pepper, to taste
1 tablespoon chopped fresh mint or basil
1 tablespoon balsamic or red wine vinegar

1. Cut zucchini diagonally into oval-shaped slices.
2. Heat oil in a large pan, and sauté zucchini slices with garlic until they are golden on both sides. Sprinkle with salt and pepper and more oil if necessary.
3. Drain fried slices on paper towels.
4. Place the zucchini slices in a bowl and scatter over them the fresh herbs and vinegar.
5. Serve at room temperature.

Serves 4

Zucchini Vinaigrette

I make this for fancy picnics and large barbecue parties.

2 lbs (1 kg) small zucchini, cut into ¼-inch (.6 cm) slices
1 small-medium red onion, chopped
1 teaspoon oregano or basil
2 oz (50 g) chopped parsley
6 fl oz (¾ cup or 180 ml) French dressing
1-2 cloves garlic, crushed

1. Cook zucchini in a large pot of boiling water for just 2 minutes. Drain immediately in a colander and rinse in cold water to stop the cooking process.
2. Place zucchini in a bowl and add onion, oregano and parsley.
3. Mix crushed garlic with the French dressing and pour over the zucchini.
4. Blend thoroughly and chill.

8 servings

Pasta Salad Sweet and Sour

*Just add small bits of cooked chicken pieces if you would like to
turn this into a main course salad.*

1 can (15 oz or 425 g) pineapple chunks
6-8 oz (175-225 g) broccoli florets
12 oz spiral-shaped pasta, cooked (or other shape)
1 medium zucchini, cubed
2 stalks celery, chopped
1-2 spring onions, chopped
½ sweet red pepper, chopped
chopped parsley

Dressing:
2 tablespoons pineapple juice
½ teaspoon garlic powder
1 tablespoon olive oil
3¼ fl oz (1/3 cup or 100 ml) white vine vinegar
2 tablespoons fresh lemon juice
2 tablespoons French mustard
2 tablespoons honey
½ teaspoon dried basil

1. Drain pineapple chunks saving 2 tablespoons of juice for
    dressing.
2. Combine all salad ingredients in a bowl.
3. Mix all dressing ingredients together. Toss the salad with the
    dressing.
4. Garnish with parsley.

Serves 8-10

Rice Salad with Zucchini and Peppers

*This colorful and filling salad looks attractive and tastes good
too.*

1 lb (500 g) rice
28 fl oz (3½ cups or 800 ml) vegetable stock
½ teaspoon ground turmeric
½ teaspoon salt
2-3 small zucchini, thinly sliced
1 red pepper, chopped
1 green pepper, chopped
3 small onions, sliced into thin rings
5 oz (140 g) black olives
8 fl oz (1 cup or 240 ml) French dressing

1. In a large pot, combine rice with vegetable stock, turmeric
   and salt. Bring to a boil, then lower heat and simmer
   covered for 20 minutes.
2. Remove lid and allow steam to escape for 5 minutes. Then
   turn rice into a large bowl and allow to cool completely.
   Chill in covered bowl and set aside until needed.
3. Mix in the zucchini, peppers, onions, and olives. Add
   dressing. Toss and mix thoroughly.

Serves 8-10

Layered Vegetable Salad

This makes a good alternative to ordinary potato salad.

4-5 medium potatoes (about 1½ lbs or 700 g)
4 fl oz (½ cup or 100 ml) red wine vinegar
2 fl oz (¼ cup or 50 ml) olive oil
1 clove garlic, crushed
1 teaspoon basil
¼ teaspoon oregano
¼ teaspoon pepper
3 tablespoon spring onions, sliced
2 tablespoons chopped parsley
salt
2 large tomatoes, sliced
2 medium zucchini, shredded

1. Cook potatoes in boiling water until just tender (about 25 minutes).
2. Make the dressing by whisking together vinegar, oil, garlic, basil, oregano and pepper. Add onions, parsley and salt.
3. Slice the cooled potatoes ¼ inch (.6 cm) thick.
4. Layer half the potatoes, tomatoes and zucchini in a serving bowl and ladle half the dressing over the layer. Make another layer with the remaining vegetables and top with remaining dressing.
5. Cover. Chill before serving.

Serves 6-8

Pickled Zucchini

*Why not? After all, pickled cucumbers were invented because a
plentiful harvest allowed them to be kept for winter usage.*

**2 lbs (nearly 1 kg) small zucchini, about 1 inch (2.5 cm) in
     diameter**
12 oz (¾ lb or 350 g) small onions, sliced into thin rounds
2 oz (50 g) pickling salt
16 fl oz (2 cups or 450 ml) cider vinegar
8 oz (1 cup or 225 g) sugar
2 tablespoons yellow mustard seeds
1 tablespoon celery seeds
1 teaspoon ground turmeric

1. Slice zucchini into ¼ inch (.6 cm) rounds and place in a
    bowl together with the onion. Mix in the salt. Cover the
    vegetables with ice cubes and allow to stand for 2 hours.
    Drain well.
2. Combine vinegar, sugar, and spices in a saucepan and bring
    to a boil. Add vegetables and bring them slowly to a boil,
    stirring frequently. Reduce heat and simmer 5 minutes.
3. Ladle vegetables and liquid into warmed-up preserving jars
    with an airtight seal, packing vegetables loosely and leaving
    a ½-inch (1.2 cm) space at top. Close and secure jars with a
    good seal.
4. Store them in a cool, dry place for at least 3 weeks before
    using.

Makes about 3-4 pints

Zucchini Chutney

This recipe will not only help to deplete your bumper crop, but will allow you to use bruised zucchini, as long as you cut away any spoiled or rotten parts. I freeze mine in small containers for convenient usage the year round.

2 lbs (1 kg) zucchini, chopped
3 lbs (1.5 kg) tomatoes, chopped
1½ lbs (700 g) onions, sliced
2 cloves garlic, chopped
20 fl oz (2½ cups or 600 ml) vinegar
1 teaspoon salt
1 teaspoon mustard
1 teaspoon red or cayenne pepper
1 tablespoon paprika
1 lb (450 g) brown sugar
4 oz (110 g) raisins

1. In a large pot, heat the zucchini, tomatoes, onions, and garlic with half the vinegar and simmer uncovered until vegetables are soft, about 30 minutes.
2. Add the rest of the vinegar and all the remaining ingredients. Simmer for about 1 hour, stirring occasionally to prevent sticking. It should be thick and reduced to a pulp, with no watery juices left. Pour into jars with airtight seal. Or freeze.

Yield: 5 lbs (2.5 kg)

Appetizers

Crudités with Vinaigrette

This healthy starter is a good choice for dinner parties and works well at finger buffets.

Vegetables:
zucchini, carrots, celery, cucumber cut into thin sticks
green, red, yellow peppers cut into strips
broccoli, cut into spears
cauliflower cut into small florets

Vinaigrette Dip:
1 teaspoon French (Dijon) mustard
5 oz (150 ml) oil
4 tablespoons wine vinegar
1 clove garlic, minced
salt
freshly ground black pepper

1. Arrange a selection of any of the crisp raw vegetables, as suggested above, on a serving platter.
2. Serve with a dip such as this vinaigrette, which can be made up and kept in a large container. Simply combine all the ingredients in a small jar, cover tightly, and shake well to mix thoroughly.

Zucchini Appetizer Salad

Another attractive salad variation that makes a good appetizer.

Salad:
8 small zucchini
lettuce leaves
2 medium tomatoes, peeled
  and chopped
½ small green pepper,
  chopped
3 tablespoons spring onions,
  finely chopped
1 tablespoon capers,
  chopped
1 tablespoon parsley,
  chopped

1 teaspoon basil
½ teaspoon oregano

Dressing:
4 fl oz (120 ml or ½ cup)
  fresh lemon juice
4 fl oz (120 ml or ½ cup)
  olive oil
l large garlic clove, minced
salt and pepper

1. Make the dressing by combining ingredients in a jar which can be shaken to mix thoroughly. Set aside.
2. Steam whole unpeeled zucchini for about 3-4 minutes. Rinse in cold water to stop further cooking. Drain.
3. Cut each zucchini in half lengthwise and scoop out the pulp. Place the zucchini shells, cut sides up, in a flat dish. Pour half the dressing over them and allow to marinate in refrigerator for at least 4 hours.
4. When ready to serve, remove zucchini (discarding the marinade) and place them, cut side up, on lettuce leaves which have been arranged on a serving platter.
5. Mix salad ingredients with the other half of the dressing and pour into the hollow zucchini shells, allowing the dressing to spill over and around.

Serves 8

Carpaccio Zucchini

An elegant but easy appetizer to make when you have a glut from the garden.

3 small zucchini (about 1 lb or 450 g)
4 fl oz (120 ml) olive oil
1 tablespoon fresh lemon juice
salt and pepper, to taste
2 oz (50 g) Parmesan cheese

1. Cut the zucchini lengthwise into very thin slices with a sharp knife or a food processor. Arrange slightly overlapping slices on a serving platter.
2. Whisk together the oil, lemon juice, and salt and pepper in a small bowl. Trickle the mixture over the zucchini.
3. Strew thinly-shaved slices of cheese over the zucchini and serve.

4 servings

Zucchini Paté

This excellent first course is enhanced by the tomato vinaigrette accompaniment, which simply blends ingredients together, and further enhanced when made a day ahead of time.

2 lbs (1 kg) zucchini, sliced
2 large onions, chopped
3 tablespoons olive oil
1 teaspoon cornstarch (or flour)
6 oz (175 g) fresh white breadcrumbs
1 tablespoon fresh basil leaves, cut up
1 tablespoon fresh tarragon
dash of nutmeg
salt and pepper to taste
3 eggs, beaten
butter

Tomato Vinaigrette Sauce (optional):
4 tomatoes
6 tablespoons olive oil
2 tablespoons red wine vinegar
salt and pepper

1. Heat oil in a large frying pan and sauté the zucchini and onions. When soft, add cornstarch and blend it all together in a food processor, not too smoothly.
2. Turn the mixture into a bowl. Add breadcrumbs, basil, tarragon, nutmeg, salt and pepper. Add beaten eggs and mix all together.
3. Put the mixture into a well-buttered paté or loaf tin, about 12 x 4 inches (30 x 12 cm).

41

4. Bake for 1 hour in a 350°F (180°C) oven.
5. Let cool and refrigerate until a half hour before ready to serve. Remove and slice the paté.
6. To make the vinaigrette, peel, remove seeds, and chop the tomatoes. Blend the ingredients together. Serve separately.

Serves 8

Ratatouille

This highly flavored Mediterranean vegetable stew is popular in French provincial cooking and may be eaten hot—or cold as an appetizer. Eggplants can be made less bitter by sprinkling with salt and allowing juices to drain away in a colander for 30 minutes.

4 tablespoons olive oil
1 large onion, chopped
4 large cloves garlic,
  minced
1 small eggplant, peeled
  and cubed
2 medium green or red
  peppers, cut into strips
3 tablespoons red wine
1 bay leaf
1 teaspoon dried basil
1 teaspoon marjoram

½ teaspoon oregano
salt and pepper, to taste
2 medium zucchini,
  thinly sliced
5 medium tomatoes,
  skinned and cut into
  chunks
4 oz (½ cup or 120 ml)
  tomato juice or water (if
  needed)
1 tablespoon capers
  (optional)

1. Heat olive oil in a pot. Add onion and garlic; sauté until onion is transparent, about 5 minutes.
2. Add eggplant, peppers, wine, and seasonings. Mix well. Cover and simmer until vegetables are tender, about 15 minutes.
3. Add zucchini and tomatoes. Continue to simmer, covered, a further 30 minutes or longer, until all vegetables are very tender. (Add tomato juice or water as needed.)
4. Add capers, if you want to, during the last 15 minutes of cooking.
5. Chill to serve as an appetizer.

Serves 6

Zucchini à la Grecque

*Here is another recipe that is equally good eaten hot (as a
vegetable accompaniment to a main course) or cold (as a first
course served on lettuce leaves).*

5-6 tablespoons olive oil
2 large onions, thinly sliced
2 large cloves of garlic, crushed
8 small-medium zucchini, sliced into rounds
6 medium tomatoes, skinned, seeded, and chopped
1 tablespoon lemon juice
1 tablespoon fresh chopped tarragon (or 1 teaspoon dried)
pinch of thyme
salt
freshly ground black pepper

1. Heat the oil in a frying pan. Sauté the onions until they are
   soft and transparent.
2. Add the minced garlic to the pan together with the sliced
   zucchini (about ½ inch or 1 cm thick) and cook for a few
   minutes.
3. Add the tomatoes and lemon juice.
4. Mix in tarragon, thyme and salt and pepper to taste.
5. Simmer gently for about 45 minutes.

Serves 8

Zucchini Fritters

This makes a delicious warm appetizer snack but can also go well as a hot side dish with grilled meat.

1/8 oz (2-3 g) fresh yeast or ½ teaspoon dried
pinch of salt
1 teaspoon warm water
2 teaspoons olive oil
2 oz (60 g) or 6 level tablespoons plain flour
1 egg white
2 small-medium zucchini, thinly sliced
oil for deep frying

1. First make the batter by placing yeast, salt and warm water into a preheated mixing bowl. When the yeast and salt are dissolved, add the oil and flour. Work the mixture together with your fingers. Cover and allow to stand for two hours in a warm place.
2. Slice zucchini thinly.
3. Heat oil in a deep fryer to 375°F (190°C).
4. Beat the egg white until stiff and fold into the batter mixture when it is ready. Coat the zucchini slices in batter and fry in the hot oil until golden brown. Remove and drain on paper towels. Serve right away.

Serves 4

Fried Zucchini Appetizer

This version of a fritter appetizer is made without yeast.

1 lb (450 g) zucchini
flour
salt and freshly ground black pepper
oil for deep-frying
2 egg whites

1. Cut zucchini into strips. Sprinkle with salt and allow to stand for 30 minutes. Rinse, drain, and dry on paper towels.
2. Heat oil until a crumb put into it sizzles actively.
3. Toss zucchini in flour seasoned with salt and pepper. Then coat them in the egg whites which have been whisked until stiff but not quite dry.
4. Fry until they are brown. Drain on paper towels, season with salt and pepper, and serve immediately.

Serves 4

Zucchini and Mushrooms in Soy Sauce

Here is another recipe that can also be used as a cold first course or a hot main course accompaniment and will go a long way toward decreasing a zucchini crop bonanza.

10 small zucchini
2 oz (50 g) butter
8 oz (225 g) mushrooms, sliced
2 tablespoons soy sauce
10 fl oz (300 ml) light cream
salt and freshly ground black pepper

1. Cut the zucchini into 1-inch (2.5 cm) slices.
2. Melt the butter in a shallow pan. Add zucchini to the melted butter and cook over low heat for about 15 minutes, stirring occasionally.
3. Add sliced mushrooms, soy sauce, cream, and salt and pepper.
4. Raise the heat and cook with the cream boiling for 5 minutes.
5. Cool and serve as a cold appetizer. Or transfer to a heated dish and serve as a side vegetable.

Serves 8

Zucchini Parmesan

Hard and pungent Parmesan cheese can be grated in the food processor. Simply cut the cheese into cubes before processing. Served at room temperature, these zucchini strips are a fine appetizer.

4 small zucchini
2 oz (¼ cup or 50 g) bread crumbs
3 oz (1/3 cup or 75 g) freshly grated Parmesan cheese
½ teaspoon dried rosemary
1/8 teaspoon red or cayenne pepper
½ teaspoon salt
¼ teaspoon freshly ground pepper
1 egg
oil

1. Cut each zucchini in half lengthwise and cut in half lengthwise again. Cut the strips in half across the width..
2. In a shallow dish, combine bread crumbs, Parmesan cheese, rosemary, and spices. Blend well.
3. In another shallow dish, beat the egg lightly. Dip each zucchini piece first in the egg and then in the cheese mixture, coating evenly.
4. Place them in a single layer on a lightly-oiled baking tray. Bake in a preheated oven at 400°F (200°C) for 5 to 7 minutes. Turn over and bake a further 5 minutes or until crisp and lightly browned.
5. Remove from oven and serve.

4 servings

Marinated Zucchini and Eggplant

A pleasant first course to prepare in advance.

3 small-medium (about 1 lb or 450 g) zucchini
1 lb (450 g) eggplant
salt and freshly ground pepper
olive oil
8 oz (240 ml) white wine vinegar
4 tablespoons white wine
juice of 1 lemon
1 carrot, diced
1 large onion, chopped
5 sage leaves, cut into small pieces
3 juniper berries
2 sprigs parsley, chopped
1 bay leaf

1. Cut zucchini and eggplant into quarters lengthways.
2. Sprinkle with salt, place in a colander, and allow to stand for 30 minutes.
3. Rinse and dry them and fry in olive oil until lightly browned. As they become tender, remove them to a baking dish, skin side up. (The eggplants need more time than the zucchini to cook.)
4. Combine remaining ingredients in a large saucepan. Bring to a boil, then lower heat and simmer for 2 minutes.
5. Pour the hot vinegar marinade over the cooked vegetables. Cover and refrigerate for 2 days.
6. Remove bay leaf and serve at room temperature.

8 servings

Zucchini Timbales

A timbale is a custard-like dish (of vegetables in this case) baked in a drum-shaped mold or ramekin.

1 lb (450 g) zucchini, grated
salt
2 eggs plus 1 egg yolk
2 oz (50 g) fresh fine white breadcrumbs
10 fl oz (1¼ cups or 300 ml) milk
l tablespoon fresh thyme, chopped
freshly ground pepper
salt to taste

1. Grate zucchini and sprinkle with salt. Allow to stand in a colander for half an hour. Rinse and dry well on paper towels.
2. Grease well (with oil) 6 ramekin dishes and set aside.
3. Beat together the eggs and egg yolk. Add the grated zucchini and the rest of the ingredients and mix well.
4. Spoon the mixture into the prepared ramekin dishes. Cover with lightly oiled greaseproof paper. Place in a large pan of water (or a bain-marie) in an oven preheated to 325°F (170°C) and bake until the timbales are set, about 40 minutes. Serve warm.

Serves 6

Mediterranean Vegetables with Tahini

This is an easy starter because it can be prepared in advance. Tahini, a paste made from sesame seeds, combines with the grilled vegetables to create a festive first course.

2 zucchini, cut in half lengthways
2 peppers, seeded and cut into quarters
2 small eggplants, cut in half lengthways
1 fennel bulb, cut into quarters
olive oil
salt and pepper to taste

Tahini sauce:
8 oz (1 cup or 225 g) tahini paste
2 cloves garlic, minced
2 tablespoons olive oil
2 tablespoons lemon juice
4 fl oz (½ cup or 120 ml) cold water

1. Brush vegetables with oil. Grill or barbecue just until they brown, turning them over once. (Peel off the skin if the peppers blacken.)
2. Season with salt and freshly ground black pepper and leave them to cool.
3. Make tahini sauce by mixing all ingredients except water in a food processor. Then, add water while motor is running, continuing to process until the mixture is smooth.
4. Arrange vegetables on a platter and dribble sauce over it. Serve at room temperature with pitta bread.

Serves 4

Hummus with Zucchini

This Middle Eastern rendition adds to the enormous variety of ways to serve zucchini. It can also use fried eggplant slices.

1 can chick peas
2 cloves garlic
6 tablespoons lemon juice
4 tablespoons tahini paste
5 tablespoons olive oil
1 teaspoon ground cumin
salt and freshly ground black pepper, to taste
1 lb (450 g) small zucchini, unpeeled
paprika

1. Drain the chick peas, setting the liquid aside, and blend them in a food processor together with the garlic until you have a smooth paste. Add some liquid from the tin if necessary.
2. Add the lemon juice and tahini and continue to process until smooth. Then, while still processing, add 3 tablespoons of the olive oil.
3. Add the cumin and salt and pepper. Mix. Transfer the smooth mixture into a covered bowl until ready to use.
4. Cut the unpeeled small zucchini lengthways into halves. In a large frying pan, heat the remaining oil and fry the zucchini, sprinkled with salt and pepper, until just tender, about 2-3 minutes on each side.
5. Arrange the zucchini on four plates and heap a portion of hummus, garnished with paprika, on each plate. Serve with pitta bread.

Serves 4

Zucchini Bruschetta

The medley of herbs enlivens the zucchini and produces this
excellent and zesty treat to whet the appetite.

4-6 small zucchini (about 1 ½ lbs or 700 g)
4 tablespoons olive oil
2 cloves garlic, crushed
1 tablespoon shredded fresh basil
1 tablespoon chopped fresh parsley
½ teaspoon oregano
salt and pepper
8 crostini (thin and lightly toasted slices of French or Italian
  bread)
about 3 oz (80 g) Swiss or other hard cheese, thinly sliced

1. Cut zucchini into strips about the size of french fries.
2. Add zucchini to oil that has been heated in a large frying
   pan and cook over medium heat for about 10 minutes,
   stirring occasionally. When lightly browned, add garlic,
   basil, parsley, and oregano. Sprinkle in some salt and a few
   grinds of pepper. Cook for 2 more minutes, stirring
   frequently. Remove from heat.
3. Spoon the zucchini mixture onto bread slices that have been
   arranged on a baking sheet. Cover with a slice of cheese and
   bake in preheated oven at 400°F (200°C), just until the
   cheese melts, about 4-5 minutes. Serve right away.

Serves 4

Fried Stuffed Zucchini Flowers

The zucchini plant produces female flowers, from which the fruit grows, and non-fruit-bearing male flowers. The flower is edible and delicious when fried or used in other dishes.

3 oz (½ cup or 80 g) flour
1 tablespoon olive oil
12 tightly closed zucchini flowers, washed and dried
1 oz (¼ cup or 25 g) coarse bread crumbs
6 anchovy fillets, mashed
1 tablespoon chopped parsley
oil for deep frying
salt and pepper to taste

1. Mix together the flour and oil and add just enough water to produce a batter that is not too liquid.
2. Remove the central piece or pistil from the zucchini flowers.
3. Soak bread crumbs in milk and squeeze them dry. Mix them together with the anchovies and parsley. Stuff the flowers with the mixture, pressing to close the flower around the filling.
4. Preheat oil to 350°F (180°C). Coat stuffed flowers with batter and deep fry them until golden all over.
5. Season with salt and pepper, drain on paper towels, and serve immediately.

Serves 4

Italian Zucchini Flowers

Italians stuff the exquisite zucchini flowers with mozzarella, coat them in a light batter, and fry them in hot olive oil.

12 fresh zucchini flowers
2 eggs
¼ teaspoon salt
8 fl oz (1 cup or 240 ml) water
8 oz (1¼ cups or 200 g) flour
mozzarella

1. Choose a fresh bunch of a dozen flowers. Carefully remove hard central piece. Do not wash. Pat dry any moisture.
2. To make the batter, beat eggs with salt and pour in water and flour. Mix well to a smooth consistency.
3. Place a thin strip of mozzarella cheese inside each flower, and dip in the batter.
4. Fry in oil that is hot but not smoking until golden and crispy. Drain on paper towels and serve immediately.

Serves 4 or 6

Baked Stuffed Zucchini Flowers

If you're intrigued with zucchini flowers, here's one version of the delicate flower that makes a gorgeous luxury and insures good dinner conversation.

12 zucchini flowers
1 ½ oz (40 g) pine nuts
1 ½ oz (40 g) breadcrumbs
6 mushrooms, finely chopped
a few tarragon leaves, chopped (optional)
1-2 tablespoons white wine
salt and pepper
2-3 tablespoons walnut or hazelnut oil

1. Open up the flower and carefully take out the hard central piece, the pistil.
2. Mix pine nuts, breadcrumbs, and mushrooms. Add tarragon if you want to. Moisten the mixture with a little white wine.
3. Use your fingers to gently fill the flowers with the stuffing mixture.
4. Lay them in a baking dish. Sprinkle with salt and pepper and brush with some of the oil.
5. Bake in a moderate oven at 350°F (180°C) for about 12 minutes. Pour remaining oil over the baked flowers and serve.

Serves 6

Lunch or Supper

Pisto

*You may scramble lightly beaten eggs into it, stirring as if making scrambled eggs, to change its designation from Spanish to French as it yields a **pipérade**.*

4 tablespoons olive oil
1 medium onion, finely chopped
2 cloves garlic, crushed
2 tablespoons fresh chopped parsley (or 1 teaspoon dry)
4 red or green peppers, sliced and seeded
1 lb (450 g) small zucchini, peeled and chopped
1 lb (450 g) tomatoes, chopped
½ lb (225 g) new potatoes, cooked
salt and pepper

1. Heat the oil in a pan and add the onion, garlic, and parsley. Cover and cook gently until onions are limp.
2. Add the peppers and continue to cook in a covered pan for another 10 minutes.
3. Add the chopped zucchini and tomatoes and continue cooking slowly, covered, for another 20 minutes.
4. Mix in the cubed potatoes, which have been separately fried in olive oil until golden and tender but not too soft. Cook for a further 10 minutes.
5. Season with salt and pepper and serve.

Serves 4

Zucchini Omelet

Other vegetables can be used in place of, or in addition to, the ones mentioned.

4 eggs
1 tablespoon butter or 1 oz (25 g) olive oil or half and half
1 or 2 small zucchini
quarter of a fresh green pepper
3 medium mushrooms
1-2 spring onions, chopped
salt and pepper to taste

1. Whisk the eggs for a few seconds. Add a dash of water (about ½ oz or 12 g) and stir. Set aside.
2. Slice peeled zucchini thinly and also cut green pepper, mushrooms, and spring onions into thin slices.
3. Melt butter and/or olive oil in a 10-inch (25 cm) omelet pan (if unavailable, use a non-stick frying pan). When butter starts to sizzle, add the slices of zucchini, mushrooms, and green peppers. Turn down the heat slightly. Stir the vegetables. Just when they start to turn brown, add a bit more olive oil if necessary, and pour in the egg mixture. Add the pieces of spring onion and sprinkle spices liberally over the entire mixture.
4. As the omelet starts to form, carefully lift one edge of the omelet and tilt the pan so that the uncooked egg runs under the cooked portion. Do this in as many places as necessary until all of the egg has formed. Fold the omelet in half. Reduce heat and carefully turn the folded omelet over so that the upper side is now in contact with the pan. Let it cook for another 30 seconds and then divide in half and serve hot.

Serves 2

Zucchini Pancake

An easy vegetable treat to go well with salad or a simple course such as grilled chicken.

2 medium zucchini, grated and squeezed dry
1 small potato, peeled and grated
1 small onion, grated
1 clove garlic, minced
2 tablespoons flour
2 eggs, slightly beaten
salt and pepper
2 teaspoons butter (sunflower oil may be substituted)
1 tablespoon fresh Parmesan cheese (optional)

1. Grate zucchini, potato, onion, and garlic in a food processor and combine them in a bowl together with the flour, eggs, and salt and pepper to taste.
2. Melt 1 teaspoon of the butter in a 10-inch (25 cm) non-stick frying pan over moderate heat.
3. Put the zucchini mixture in the pan, shaping it with a spatula. Cook, uncovered, over medium heat until the edges are golden and the bottom is firm and crisp (10-12 minutes). Turn over by placing a large plate over the pan and inverting the pancake onto it.
4. Melt the remaining butter in the pan, and slide the pancake back into the pan. Cook until firm (about 8-10 minutes).
5. Sprinkle with Parmesan cheese, if you want to, and serve.

Serves 4

Zucchini-Carrot Kugel

*This recipe will add further proof—if further proof is needed—
that zucchini is not a tedious or uninteresting vegetable.*

3-4 medium zucchini, coarsely grated
3 medium onions, finely chopped
3 tablespoons butter
5 medium carrots, coarsely grated
3 large eggs, beaten
3½-4 oz (¾ cup or 110 g) matzo meal or fine breadcrumbs
6 tablespoons flour
1 teaspoon baking powder
freshly ground black pepper
2 tablespoons butter for dotting the top

1. Salt zucchini and allow to stand in a colander for 30 to 40 minutes. Squeeze out remaining water.
2. In a heavy pan sauté the onion in butter over medium heat until limp and transparent (about 5 minutes). Remove from heat.
3. Turn sautéed onions into a large bowl and mix together with the grated zucchini and grated carrots.
4. Add the beaten eggs and the matzo meal (or breadcrumbs).
5. Sift in the flour and baking powder, and grind in black pepper. Mix well.
6. Turn the batter into a well-greased 9x13 inch (23x31 cm) baking pan. Scatter small bits of butter on the top.
7. Bake in oven preheated to 375°F (190°C) for 1¼ hours.

Serves 4-6

Zucchini-Carrot Latkes

These latkes, or pancakes, which will perk up any repast, can be made in advance. When ready to serve, place them on a baking sheet and heat them in a 400°F (200°C) oven.

4 large zucchini, shredded
4 large carrots, shredded
2-3 spring onions, chopped
4 eggs, beaten
4 oz (½ cup or 110 g) flour
2 teaspoons baking powder
½ teaspoon nutmeg
pinch of cardamom
salt and pepper, to taste
oil for frying, preferably peanut oil

1. Shred the carrots and zucchini in a food processor and place in a large bowl. Add the spring onions and beaten eggs. Blend it all together.
2. Add the flour, baking powder, nutmeg, cardamom, salt and pepper. Mix well.
3. Heat oil in a large frying pan. Drop the mixture by spoonfuls into the oil. When pancakes are set, turn them over, and continue to fry until they are crisp. Remove them and place on absorbent paper towels to remove any excess oil and serve.

Serves 6

Frittata of Zucchini

Serve this quick supper or lunch with a green salad and crusty bread.

1 tablespoon olive oil
4 medium zucchini, thinly sliced
1 red pepper, cut into thin slices
1-2 cloves garlic, chopped
6 eggs, lightly beaten
4 tablespoons sun-dried tomatoes, drained of oil and
  chopped
2-3 spring onions, chopped
2 tablespoons fresh basil or mint or a mixture of both
salt and pepper
1 oz (25 g) grated cheese such as cheddar

1. Heat oil in a large frying pan and cook the zucchini, red pepper, and garlic for about 10 minutes, until soft. Stir occasionally.
2. Whisk the eggs in a bowl and add tomatoes, spring onions, herbs and seasonings. Mix it all together.
3. Reduce heat under the pan and pour in the egg mixture, allowing it to run under the vegetables. Cook over a low heat until the base is golden.
4. Sprinkle cheese over the top and place the pan under preheated hot grill until the cheese melts. Cut into wedges.

Serves 6-8

Zucchini Soufflé

Soufflés are not necessarily tricky or difficult, and this one could become a great favorite. It can be prepared in advance up to step 3. Then, when ready to serve, reheat gently before folding in the whipped egg whites.

2 tablespoons breadcrumbs	salt and pepper
2 small zucchini (about 14 oz or 400 g)	¼ teaspoon nutmeg
	4 egg yolks
4 tablespoons butter	6 tablespoons cheddar
1 onion, finely chopped	3 tablespoons Parme-
3 tablespoons flour	san cheese, grated
6 fl oz (¾ cup or 180 ml) milk	6 egg whites
4 fl oz (½ cup or 120 ml) cream	

1. Cook zucchini for just a few minutes, until tender; drain, chop and purée them in a blender or food processor.
2. Cook the onion in melted butter until soft. Add flour and cook another 2 minutes. Add milk, cream, and zucchini purée. Stir in salt and pepper to taste and nutmeg.
3. Remove from heat and beat in the egg yolks together with the cheddar and Parmesan. (Stop here if you are preparing in advance.)
4. Beat the egg whites until stiff and fold into the mixture.
5. Pour the mixture into 8 ramekin dishes which have been buttered and sprinkled with breadcrumbs. Sprinkle a little extra Parmesan cheese over the ramekins.
6. Bake at 400°F oven (200°C) for 12-15 minutes.

Serves 8

Vegetable Quiche

Ingredients can be varied according to what you have available in your garden.

pastry
2 tablespoons olive oil
1 large onion, chopped
2 cloves garlic, minced
3 zucchini, sliced
4 carrots, sliced
4 oz (100 g) peas
1 lb ((450 g) mushrooms,
  sliced

1 tablespoon tamari (or
  Japanese soy sauce)
12 oz (350 g) cheddar or
  other hard cheese,
  grated
7 eggs
5 fl oz (150 ml) milk
salt and pepper, to taste
3 tablespoons light cream

1. Line a greased flan dish with pastry.
2. Heat the oil in a pan and sauté all vegetables except mushrooms. When onions have softened, add mushrooms and cook a few minutes longer.
3. Remove from heat. Add tamari and blend ingredients together.
4. Fill the pastry-lined flan dish with half the cheese, then vegetables, then the rest of the cheese.
5. In a large bowl, beat the eggs together with the milk, and season with salt and pepper. Pour this mixture over all. Then slowly decant the cream into the middle of the quiche.
6. Bake at 275°F (140°C) for 50 minutes, until the color is golden and the center is firm.

Serves 6

Zucchini Pudding

This is a popular dairy dish of the Eastern Mediterranean that is also good served cold in the summertime.

4 zucchini (about 2 lbs or 1 kg)
3 eggs, beaten
½ lb (225 g) coarse farmer or cottage cheese
½ teaspoon salt
2 oz (¼ cup or 50 g) herbed breadcrumbs
butter

1. Peel the zucchini and grate coarsely.
2. Mix zucchini with beaten eggs, cheese, salt and bread-crumbs.
3. Turn the mixture into a well-buttered baking dish, 8 x 8 inches (20 x 20 cm).
4. Bake in a 350°F (180°C) oven for a half hour or until brown.
5. Cut into squares and serve warm.

Serves 4

Vegetable Kebabs

Here's one that can be done on the outside barbecue with a variety of fresh vegetables from the garden. Serve on a bed of rice with garlic bread for a pleasant summer supper.

2 zucchini, cut into 1-inch (3 cm) slices
2 yellow zucchini, cut into 1-inch (3 cm) slices
2 large green peppers, cut into 1-inch (3 cm) squares
2 large red sweet peppers, cut into 1-inch (3 cm) squares
1 medium onion, quartered
1 bottle Italian salad dressing

1. Place vegetables in a bowl and add Italian dressing. Mix well and marinate for an hour.
2. Remove vegetables from marinade, reserving marinade, and thread them alternately on skewers.
3. Place skewers of kebabs on the grate and cook for 10 to 15 minutes, brushing with marinade during cooking and turning once halfway through.

Serves 4

Stuffed Pasta Shells

Serve with a salad to make a satisfying, calorie-conscious Italian repast.

6 oz (175 g) jumbo shells, uncooked
15 oz (1 ¾ cups or 425 g) low-fat ricotta cheese
4 oz (1 cup or 100-125 g) shredded low-fat mozzarella cheese
3 tablespoons grated Parmesan cheese
1 unpeeled medium zucchini, finely shredded and drained
1 carrot, finely shredded
few sprigs of flat leaf parsley, chopped
1 clove garlic, minced
½ teaspoon oregano
salt and pepper, to taste
16 oz (450 g) tomato sauce

1. Cook pasta shells according to directions on package. Drain and place them separately on a plate or waxed paper to prevent them from sticking together.
2. Combine remaining ingredients, except tomato sauce, in a bowl. Mix well.
3. Fill each pasta shell with about 1½ tablespoons of this mixture.
4. Cover the bottom of a 6 x 10 inch (15 x 25 cm) baking dish with a thin spread of some of the sauce. Arrange shells in the dish, cheese side up. Spoon remaining sauce over shells.
5. Cover and bake in 350°F (180°C) oven for 35 minutes.

6 servings

Zucchini Boats

Shirley, who gave me this recipe, often prepares it ahead of time or freezes it for future use. For a complete meal, serve with a salad and wholelmeal bread and butter.

4 large zucchini (about ½ lb or 225 g each)
2 large onions, finely chopped
2 stalks of celery, chopped
2-3 garlic cloves, minced
2 tablespoons olive oil
l large tin of tomatoes
bunch of freshly chopped parsley
salt and pepper, to taste
2 oz (50 g) grated cheese

1. Steam the washed but unpeeled zucchini for five minutes.
2. Split them lengthwise. Scoop out the soft yellow centers, chop finely, and put aside. Place the zucchini boats in a baking dish.
3. Fry the chopped onions and celery and the minced garlic in olive oil.
4. Add the chopped zucchini pulp to the pan. Add the tin of chopped tomatoes (or fresh tomatoes) and the parsley.
5. Mix it all together and cook, stirring occasionally. Season as required.
6. Fill the zucchini boats with the mixture. Sprinkle with the grated cheese and bake at 350°F (180° C) for about 30 minutes.

Serves 4

Zucchini Ripiene

Serve this Italian version of zucchini boats with a crisp salad.

4 medium zucchini
1 medium onion
2 garlic cloves, minced
1 tablespoon olive oil
2 tomatoes
1 teaspoon finely chopped oregano leaves
salt and pepper to taste
Parmesan cheese
breadcrumbs

1. Wash the zucchini and split lengthwise. Steam for five minutes, then scoop out the center pulp and chop this finely.
2. Place the boat-shaped zucchini cases in a baking dish.
3. Fry the finely-chopped onion and garlic in olive oil together with the zucchini pulp for 5 minutes. Add skinned, chopped, and deseeded tomatoes, and the oregano and seasonings. Blend together and cook for a further 5 minutes.
4. Spoon the mixture into the zucchini cases, top with a layer of Parmesan cheese and sprinkle with fine breadcrumbs.
5. Bake for 15 minutes in preheated oven at 375°F (190° C).

Serves 4

Mediterranean Zucchini Bake

A vegetarian course that combines ingredients and flavors to create an attractive and tasty dish.

4 medium zucchini, about 2 lbs (900 g)
4 eggs
½-1 teaspoon salt
¼ teaspoon freshly ground black pepper
8 oz (1½ cups or 225 g) fine bread crumbs
7 oz (1 cup or 200 g) freshly grated Parmesan cheese
a handful of fresh basil leaves, cut into small pieces
2 teaspoons chopped fresh thyme, or 1 teaspoon dried thyme
2 tablespoons chopped fresh flat-leaf parsley
olive oil
1 lb (450 g) mozzarella, cut into thin slices
2-3 medium tomatoes, thinly sliced

1. Cut zucchini lengthwise into very thin slices.
2. In a bowl, beat the eggs lightly. Add salt and pepper and set aside.
3. In another bowl mix together the bread crumbs, Parmesan cheese, basil, thyme, and parsley and set aside.
4. Oil the bottom of a 12 x 14-inch (30 x 36 cm) baking dish. Arrange a layer of zucchini slices on the bottom, followed by a layer of mozzarella, then a layer of tomato slices. Sprinkle over it some of the bread crumb mixture and drizzle lightly with olive oil. Repeat the layers until all the vegetables are used up, ending with a layer of mozzarella. Pour the egg mixture evenly over the top.

5. Bake in a preheated oven at 350° F (180°C) for about 45 minutes or until the eggs are set and the top is golden. If it starts browning too quickly, cover with aluminum foil and remove the foil for the last 5 minutes of baking.
6. Allow it to settle for 10 minutes after removing from the oven. Then cut into squares. May be served warm or cold.

Serves 6-8

Risotto with Spring Vegetables

Although risotto is easy to cook, you need to watch it. Stirring almost constantly while gradually adding wine, rice and vegetables yields a moist, yet slightly nutty result. Besides, how can it be bad with all that wine?

4 oz (125 g) butter, divided into quarters
2 medium onions, finely chopped
2 large cloves garlic, finely chopped
1 medium zucchini, cut into small pieces
4 oz (1 cup or 110 g) fresh green peas
2 carrots, diced
1 tomato, peeled and cut into small pieces
16 fl oz (2 cups or 450 ml) dry white wine
l lb (450 g) Italian Arborio or short grain rice
48 fl oz (6 cups or 1.4 litres) boiling stock
2 oz (½ cup or 50 g) finely grated Italian cheese such as parmigiano or romano
salt and freshly ground pepper

1. Melt 1 quarter of the butter in a small saucepan on low heat and cook half the chopped onion and garlic in it together with all of the vegetables, stirring frequently.
2. When the onion is soft and golden, add half of the wine and simmer until wine has evaporated. Set aside.
3. Melt 2 more quarters of the butter in a large pot and add the remaining onion and garlic, cooking and stirring until the onion is soft. Add the rice, stirring until it is well mixed together. Then pour in the remaining wine and stir until the wine is absorbed.

4. Add one cup of boiling stock at a time, stirring until each cupful is absorbed before adding more, until it is used up. Rice should be creamy but slightly nutty in texture and completely cooked in about 20 minutes.
5. Stir in the vegetable mixture which has been set aside. Add the remaining butter and half the cheese. Add salt and freshly ground pepper to taste.
6. Serve right away with remaining cheese served separately.

Serves 6

Spicy African Stew

The unusual blend of ingredients and flavors makes a satisfying party delight.

1 tablespoon oil
1 medium onion, chopped
1 medium sweet potato, peeled and diced
2 garlic cloves, crushed
32 fl oz (4 cups or 1 litre) chicken stock
5 ½-6 oz (¾ cup or 175 g) uncooked white rice
1 teaspoon thyme
½ teaspoon cumin
½-1 teaspoon salt
16 fl oz (2 cups or 450 ml) tomato sauce
2 16-oz (450 g) tins chickpeas, drained and rinsed
1 medium zucchini, sliced
6 oz (175 g) peanut butter

1. Heat the oil in a large pot. Sauté onion, sweet potato and garlic until the onion is tender.
2. Stir in the stock, rice, thyme, cumin, and salt and bring to a boil. Then reduce heat.
3. Simmer for 20 minutes, stirring frequently, until the rice and vegetables are tender.
4. Mix in the tomato sauce, chickpeas and zucchini. Simmer for 15 minutes, stirring occasionally, until zucchini is tender.
5. Stir in the peanut butter.
6. Ladle into soup bowls and serve with crusty French bread.

8 servings

75

Pitta with Zucchini and Carrots

Most of the preparation can be done in advance, but do not fill the pitta breads too soon or the salad mixture will make the pitta bread soggy.

2 carrots
1 oz (25 g) pecan nuts (or walnuts)
4 spring onions, sliced
2 fl oz (¼ cup or 50 ml) Greek yogurt
8 teaspoons olive oil
1 teaspoon lemon juice
1 tablespoon chopped fresh mint
2 zucchini
flour
salt and freshly ground black pepper
2 pitta breads
shredded lettuce

1. Place coarsely-grated carrots in a bowl. Add pecans and spring onions and mix well.
2. In another bowl, whisk the yogurt with 2 teaspoons of the olive oil, lemon juice, and fresh mint. Turn this dressing into the carrot mixture and toss well. Chill in a covered bowl until needed.
3. Slice the unpeeled zucchini diagonally. Season flour with salt and pepper and dip the zucchini slices in it.
4. Heat the rest of the oil in a large frying pan. Add the coated zucchini slices and fry for 3-4 minutes, turning once, until browned. Drain on paper towels.
5. Fill the slit or pocket of each pitta bread with the carrot mixture and zucchini slices. Serve on shredded lettuce.

Serves 2

Pizza with Zucchini

There are few hard and fast rules for topping ingredients, which come in infinite varieties; this recipe could be called pizza-with-anything or pizza-as-you-like-it.

basic pizza shell
tomato sauce
garlic, sliced or chopped
oregano and basil
other spices—thyme, bay leaf, fennel, parsley
salt and pepper
mozzarella cheese
2 small zucchini, sliced
other toppings—mushrooms, green pepper, onions, spinach,
   anchovies, etcetera
2 tablespoons grated Parmesan cheese
1 tablespoon olive oil

1. Parbake the crust for about 4 minutes to give the dough a spring and prevent the weight of ingredients from pressing on the dough and making it heavy.
2. Spread tomato sauce evenly over pizza base leaving only a small border. You can make your own sauce by cooking the following ingredients over low heat for about 10 minutes: 2 lbs (1 kg) ripe tomatoes; 2 tablespoons olive oil; 1 teaspoon sugar; salt. Discard watery liquid.
3. Sprinkle garlic over the sauce and add oregano and basil.
4. Sprinkle other spices over all, selecting the ones you like in the quantities you like.
5. Place mozzarella, thinly sliced, over sauce.

6. Arrange thinly-sliced zucchini over all. Add sliced mush-rooms, green pepper, onions—or whatever you select. (Add sausage or pepperoni, if you want to.)
7. Sprinkle Parmesan cheese over all.
8. Dribble olive oil over the pizza.
9. Bake in a hot oven (425°F or 220°C) for about twenty minutes or until crust is lightly browned and ingredients are cooked through.

Ciabatta Rolls with Zucchini and Tomato-Saffron Sauce

A creamy tomato sauce provides the basis for a yummy zucchini "sandwich."

1 ½ lbs (700 g) small zucchini
1 tablespoon olive oil
2 shallots, chopped
small can chopped tomatoes
pinch of sugar (optional)
a few saffron threads
2 fl oz (50 ml or ¼ cup) light cream
salt and pepper
4 ciabatta rolls

1. Cut small unpeeled zucchini in half, then cut each half lengthways into quarters to make strips about 1½ inches (4 cm) long.
2. In a large frying pan, heat the oil; add the chopped shallots and sauté over medium heat for a minute or two.
3. Put the zucchini strips into the pan and cook for 5-6 minutes, stirring frequently.
4. Stir in the tomatoes and sugar (if desired). Immerse saffron threads in a drop of hot water for a few minutes and add to the zucchini with the cream. Cook for 4 minutes, stirring occasionally. Season to taste.
5. Cut open the rolls which have been warmed, and fill them with the zucchini and sauce mixture.

Serves 4

Casseroles

Zucchini Casserole

For a relaxing dinner party, prepare this vegetarian casserole the night before and leave it in the refrigerator to await the arrival of your guests before placing it in the oven.

2 tablespoons butter
2 medium onions, sliced
4-5 small zucchini
1 tin (1 lb or 450 g) tomatoes
salt to taste
grated cheese

1. Sauté the sliced onions in melted butter until golden.
2. Place onions in a casserole mixed together with sliced zucchini. Add tomatoes (fresh cut-up tomatoes may be substituted) and salt.
3. Cover and refrigerate.
4. When ready to cook, sprinkle grated cheese over top of casserole to cover all ingredients. Bake uncovered in 350°F (180°C) oven for 30-35 minutes.

Serves 6

Marrow Casserole

*This is an excellent way to use zucchini that have become
enormous after you've been away on holiday or forgotten to pick
them. Overgrown zucchini—or marrows—have a high water
content and do not lend themselves to steaming, but they are
good baked in a casserole.*

1 marrow (approximately 2 lbs or nearly 1 kg)
1 or 2 tomatoes
1 ½ ounces (40 g) butter
2 tablespoons mixed fresh herbs—tarragon, basil, parsley,
  and chives
salt and pepper

1. Peel the marrow and cut into 1-inch (2.5 cm) thick slices;
   cut into rough chunks, discarding the seeds.
2. Add quartered tomatoes and mix with fresh, chopped herbs.
   Season with salt and freshly ground pepper.
3. Butter an ovenproof dish and add the marrow with the
   remaining butter cut into small pieces.
4. Cover the dish and bake in preheated oven at 350° F
   (180°C) until just tender, about twenty minutes. Serve from
   the dish.

Serves 4-6

83

Zucchini Cheese Casserole

Made with low-fat cottage cheese, this is another low-calorie, low-cholesterol recipe to add to your heart healthy repertory.

3 medium zucchini, sliced
1 medium onion, chopped
2 tomatoes, sliced
2 tablespoons oil
1 lb (450 g) low-fat cottage cheese
1 teaspoon basil
½ teaspoon oregano
salt
3 oz (75 g) grated Parmesan cheese

1. Sauté zucchini slices and chopped onion in oil until golden.
2. Blend the cottage cheese well with basil and oregano and salt.
3. Alternate layers of zucchini, cottage cheese mixture, and tomato in casserole, and top with parmesan cheese.
4. Bake at 350°F (180°C) for 25-30 minutes. Uncover during last 10 minutes.

Serves 6

Zucchini Parmesan Casserole

Another easy version of zucchini with Parmesan cheese.

2 medium zucchini (about 1 lb or 450 g)
1 tablespoon butter
1 teaspoon salt
1 teaspoon chopped parsley
4 tablespoons grated Parmesan cheese

1. Cut zucchini into thin slices and arrange them in a layer in a greased shallow baking dish.
2. Dot with some of the butter, and sprinkle with some of the salt, parsley and cheese.
3. Repeat layers until all ingredients are used, ending with cheese.
4. Bake in preheated oven at 400°F (200°C) for about 25 minutes, until zucchini is tender. If desired, place it under the grill just until the top is golden brown.

Serves 2-3

California Zucchini Cheese Casserole

*Why California? Perhaps because Italians emigrated to that
state and brought their familiar ingredients with them.*

4 medium-large zucchini, sliced
l large can tomatoes, about
  1 lb 12 oz (800 g or 3 ½ cups)
1 large green pepper, chopped
8 oz (225 g) mushrooms, sliced
¼ teaspoon basil
1 onion, chopped
¼ teaspoon oregano

½ teaspoon sugar (optional)
salt and pepper, to taste
12 oz (350 g) herb seasoned
  stuffing crumbs
4-6 oz (125-175 g) mozza-
  rella cheese, shredded
2 oz (50 g) Parmesan
  cheese, grated

1. Parboil the zucchini and drain.
2. In a large bowl, combine all ingredients, except cheeses. Mix together and transfer to a casserole.
3. Sprinkle cheeses over the top and bake at 350°F (180°C) for 30 minutes.

Serves 8

Spicy Zucchini and Potato Mash

This spicy side dish goes well on any North African or Middle Eastern menu.

2 medium zucchini
2 potatoes
¾ teaspoon ground cumin
¼ teaspoon chili powder
½ teaspoon caraway seed
¼ teaspoon salt
1 tablespoon lemon juice
4 garlic cloves, crushed
2 tablespoons olive oil

1. Peel the zucchini, cut them into chunks, and cook in water until they are soft (about 20 minutes). Drain and mash coarsely.
2. Cook the potatoes in water until soft. Drain and mash coarsely. Mix them both together.
3. Mix the cumin, chili (use less if you prefer a less spicy taste), caraway, salt, lemon juice, and garlic together into a paste and stir it into the vegetables.
4. Put the mixture into a lightly buttered casserole. Dribble the olive oil over the top. When ready to serve, place the casserole in a 350°F (180°C) oven to heat through.

Serves 4-6

Zucchini Custard Casserole

Accompanied by a salad, this casserole makes a rich and simple one-dish supper that is also satisfying and colorful.

1 lb (450 g) zucchini, sliced
1 tablespoon minced onion
2 tablespoons olive or sunflower oil
3 eggs
4 fl oz (½ cup or 120 ml) milk
8-10 oz (225-280 g) cheddar cheese, grated
2 tablespoons dry bread crumbs
½ teaspoon salt
dash cayenne pepper
thyme, to taste

1. In a frying pan, sauté unpeeled zucchini and onion in oil until tender. Set aside.
2. In a large bowl, beat eggs and milk. Add one third of the cheese plus the bread crumbs, salt, pepper, and thyme to milk-egg mixture. Stir in zucchini and onion.
3. Turn mixture into a greased casserole and sprinkle the top with the rest of the grated cheese.
4. Bake uncovered in 350°F (180°C) oven for 35-40 minutes.

Serves 3-4

Summer Zucchini and Mushroom Bake

Yellow (or green) zucchini may be substituted for the squash, especially if available in your overflowing vegetable garden.

1 small zucchini, cut into small cubes
1 small yellow squash, cut into small cubes
5-10 mushrooms, sliced
1 small (or ½ medium) red onion, thinly sliced
3-4 oz (80-100g) mozzarella cheese, shredded
2 tablespoons shredded fresh basil or 1 tablespoon dried
   basil
salt and pepper

1. Combine zucchini, squash, mushrooms and red onion in a casserole and mix well. Sprinkle with the cheese, basil, and salt and pepper.
2. Cover and bake at 350°F (180°C) for 25 to 30 minutes or until the vegetables are crisp.

Serves 4

Winter Stew

Perfect for cheering up an otherwise cheerless, cold-weather day.

1½-2 lbs (700-900 g) minced beef
1 small head of cabbage
1 small onion, chopped
2 stalks celery, chopped
1 large carrot, sliced
1 medium-large zucchini
1 small turnip, sliced
salt and freshly ground black pepper to taste
34 fl oz (about 4¼ cups or 1 litre) V-8 or tomato juice
8 oz (1 cup or 225 g) rice, bulgar, or barley

1. Brown the beef, drain off the fat, and put the beef in a casserole.
2. Place over it the cabbage, which has been cored and cut into small wedges, and the other vegetables. Season with salt and freshly ground black pepper.
3. Pour tomato juice over all and bake in oven at 325°F (170°C) for an hour.
4. Add the grain of your choice and more juice or water if necessary. Cook for another half hour, until grain is done.

Serves 6-8

Zucchini Orange Bake

Goes well with beef or lamb dishes.

3-4 medium zucchini
4 large tomatoes, sliced
1 medium onion, chopped
1 tablespoon olive oil
1 tablespoon white wine vinegar
1 teaspoon sugar (optional)
½ teaspoon rosemary
grated rind and juice of half an orange
salt and pepper, to taste

1. Arrange overlapping slices of tomatoes and zucchini in a casserole.
2. Combine remaining ingredients and add to casserole.
3. Cover and bake in preheated oven at 350°F (180°C) for 20-25 minutes, until vegetables are tender.

Serves 4

Vegetable Macaroni Bake

Other pasta shapes may be used instead of macaroni.

8 oz (225 g) short cut macaroni
5 tablespoons butter
1 tablespoon flour
8 fl oz (1 cup or 250 ml) milk
4 oz (100 g) grated Parmesan
  cheese
½ teaspoon dry mustard
1 clove garlic, crushed

3 carrots, peeled and diced
1 red pepper (capsicum),
  seeded and sliced
2 zucchini, thinly sliced
4 oz (100 g) mushrooms,
  sliced
1 tablespoon tomato paste
½ teaspoon dried oregano
salt and pepper

1. Cook the macaroni in boiling water until barely tender, drain and rinse.
2. Melt 3 tablespoons butter in a pan, stir in the flour and cook for about a minute. Gradually add the milk and bring to the boil, stirring until thickened. Mix in just over half the cheese and the mustard.
3. In another pan, melt the remaining butter and add the garlic and carrots. Fry gently for a few minutes, then add the red pepper and cook for 2 minutes. Add the zucchini, mushrooms, tomato paste, oregano and salt and pepper. Cook for 3 to 4 minutes.
4. Put half the macaroni in a greased ovenproof dish and spoon the vegetable mixture over it. Add about a third of the sauce, then add the rest of the macaroni and the rest of the sauce.
5. Sprinkle the remaining cheese over the top and bake in a hot oven at 400°F (200°C) for 30 to 40 minutes, until bubbling and brown. Serve hot.

Serves 4-6

Zucchini-Spaghetti Casserole

Another easy way to use zucchini in a dish that can be given more color by leaving the zucchini unpeeled. It can also be prepared ahead of time, ready to go into the oven when your guests arrive.

4 oz (110 g) uncooked spaghetti, broken
1 large onion, chopped
1 green pepper, chopped
3 oz (80 g) butter
4 medium zucchini, sliced
4 medium tomatoes, cut in wedges
3-4 tablespoons fresh chopped parsley
salt and pepper to taste
6 oz (175 g) Swiss cheese, coarsely grated

1. Put broken spaghetti in a large pot of boiling water and boil gently until barely tender. Drain.
2. In a frying pan, cook onions and pepper in butter until tender, about 4 minutes. Add zucchini, cover and cook slowly for another 5-6 minutes. Stir in tomatoes, parsley, salt and pepper. Cover and cook until heated.
3. Put the mixture into a large casserole, and gently mix in the drained spaghetti. Spread cheese over the top. Bake in a 350°F (180°C) oven for 30 to 40 minutes.

Serves 4-5

Zucchini and Potato Casserole

*Although this recipe will serve six as an accompaniment, it
could make a main meal to serve four.*

1 tablespoon olive oil
12 oz (350 g) onions, chopped
14 oz (400 g) tin of chopped tomatoes
1 teaspoon tomato paste (purée)
½ teaspoon sugar
1 tablespoon chopped parsley
salt and freshly ground black pepper, to taste
6 tablespoons water
1 lb (450 g) potatoes, thinly sliced
2 medium-large zucchini (about 1 lb or 450 g), sliced

1. Heat half the oil in a frying pan, add the onions and cook
    gently over medium heat until soft and golden.
2. Add the tomatoes, tomato purée, sugar, parsley, seasonings
    and water. Simmer for 5 minutes.
3. Layer the potatoes and zucchini in a large casserole. Pour
    tomato mixture over it.
4. Cover and bake in preheated oven at 350°F (180°C) for 1½-
    1¾ hours or until potatoes are done.

Serves 6

Italian Vegetable Casserole

This combination of colorful fresh vegetables, which forms the basis of so much Italian cooking, yields a good texture and a rich and flavorful casserole.

2 medium zucchini, sliced
1 small (about 8 oz or 225 g) eggplant
3 large tomatoes, sliced
3 tablespoons olive oil
1 oz (25 g) butter
salt and pepper
2 cloves garlic, crushed
½ teaspoon marjoram
4 oz (110 g) mozzarella cheese, thinly sliced

1. Slice eggplant thinly. Sprinkle with salt and allow to stand in a colander for 30 minutes. Rinse well and pat dry.
2. Heat olive oil and butter in a large pan and fry eggplant slices until they are soft. Arrange them in an ovenproof casserole. Then fry the zucchini in the remaining oil until they are soft. Layer zucchini and tomatoes over the eggplant. Pour any remaining pan juices over all. Season with salt and pepper. Sprinkle with garlic and marjoram.
3. Place mozzarella over the top.
4. Cover and bake in preheated oven at 350°F (180°C) for 35-45 minutes, until vegetables are tender.

Serves 4-6

Zucchini and Eggplant Crumble

Great for a bumper crop of zucchini.

3 tablespoons olive oil
2 medium red onions, sliced
2 cloves garlic, chopped
8 zucchini, sliced and cut into
  semi-circles
2 small eggplants, cut into
  cubes
1 teaspoon rosemary
1 teaspoon dried dill weed
  (or a handful of fresh)
½ teaspoon allspice
salt and pepper

10 tomatoes, chopped
2 tablespoons tomato paste
10 fl oz (300 ml) tomato
  juice
10 fl oz (300 ml) chicken or
  vegetable stock
8 oz (225 g) butter
12 oz (350 g) wholewheat
  flour
8 oz (225 g) ground walnuts
8 oz (225 g) chopped
  walnuts

1. Heat oil in large pot and sauté onion and garlic until onions are soft. Add zucchini and eggplants, herbs and spices, and continue to cook for a few minutes.
2. Add tomatoes and tomato paste. Pour in tomato juice and stock. Simmer about 15-20 minutes. When vegetables are tender, turn them into a greased casserole.
3. For the topping, rub softened butter into flour, then add ground and chopped walnuts. Spoon the mixture evenly over the top.
4. Bake at 325°F (160°C) for 40-45 minutes.

Serves 8-10

Baked Zucchini Casserole

Other vegetables—sliced new potatoes, eggplants, peppers—can also be used for the layers of this vegetarian dish.

2 lbs (nearly 1 kg) zucchini, sliced
1 medium onion, thinly sliced
14 oz (400 g) tin tomatoes
6 tablespoons olive oil
6 tablespoons vegetable or chicken stock
1 teaspoon brown sugar
2 cloves garlic, crushed
2 tablespoons parsley, chopped
salt and pepper, to taste
2 tablespoons wholemeal breadcrumbs
8-12 black pitted olives

1. Place a layer of zucchini in the bottom of a greased casserole, followed by a layer of sliced onion, then tomatoes (use fresh ones if you want to). Continue in this way until you have used up all the vegetables.
2. In a small bowl, combine 4 tablespoons of the olive oil, the stock, sugar, garlic, parsley, and salt and pepper. (Increase the amounts, if necessary, if you have used additional vegetables.) Mix well and pour over the vegetables.
3. Scatter the breadcrumbs and the rest of the oil over the top.
4. Bake in a moderate oven at 350°F (180°C) for 1 hour.
5. Garnish with black olives and serve.

Serves 4-6

Mashed Zucchini Casserole

Add leftover cooked diced chicken, if desired, to serve as a main course.

2 lbs (900 g) zucchini or marrow, cooked, drained and mashed
1 medium carrot, grated
1 medium onion, chopped
1 small can cream of chicken soup
4 oz (110 g) butter
1 small package herbed breadcrumb stuffing mix

1. Cut unpeeled zucchini into small pieces and cook in water just until soft enough to mash.
2. Mix mashed zucchini together with grated carrot, chopped onion, and soup.
3. Melt the butter and blend with the breadcrumb stuffing mix.
4. Grease a baking dish and pat three quarters of the stuffing mixture into the bottom, like a crust. Spoon the zucchini mixture over it. Sprinkle remaining crumbs over the top.
5. Bake at 350°F (180°C) for 40 minutes.

Serves 8-10

Zucchini Couscous

This simple zucchini dish is made with couscous, a grain that offers an excellent and tasty way to boost fiber intake.

1 medium zucchini, chopped
2 tablespoons chopped spring onions
2 tablespoons soy sauce
2 tablespoons white wine
1 clove garlic, crushed
4 oz (110 g) uncooked couscous
5 fl oz (150 ml) water
1½ teaspoons butter

1. Combine zucchini, spring onions, soy sauce, white wine, and garlic in a casserole and mix. Add couscous, water, and dots of butter and stir well.
2. Bake in 350°F (180°C) oven for 30 minutes. Add more water if needed.

Serves 4

Vegetable Bourguignonne

The vegetables absorb the wine and herbs to make a satisfying vegetarian dish.

2 tablespoons olive oil
3 zucchini, cut into thick slices
2 medium carrots, sliced
2 leeks, sliced
1 lb (450 g) new potatoes
12 oz (350 g) small whole onions or shallots
1 lb (450 g) small button mushrooms
1 parsnip, sliced
3 celery stalks, sliced
2 bay leaves
3 tablespoons wholewheat flour
14 fl oz (1 ¾ cups or 400 ml) red wine
2 tablespoons tomato paste (purée)
2 tablespoons lemon juice
1 tablespoon dried sage
salt to taste
12 oz (350 g) grated hard cheese such as cheddar

1. Sauté vegetables in oil together with bay leaves for 20 minutes.
2. Stir in flour and cook for a minute. Then blend in wine, tomato paste, lemon juice, sage, and salt.
3. Turn into a casserole and bake at 300°F (150° C) for about 50 minutes, until vegetables are tender.
4. During last 10 minutes sprinkle with cheese.

Serves 6

Main Courses

Neapolitan Zucchini and Eggplant with Pasta

My vegetarian friends appreciate this satisfying and substantial dish.

8 oz (225 g) pasta shells
2 medium onions, sliced
3 large cloves garlic, sliced
3 red peppers, cut into strips
4 tablespoons olive oil, plus a
  little more for the topping
2 eggplants, diced
2 bay leaves
salt

1 teaspoon marjoram
1 teaspoon thyme
6 small zucchini, sliced
12 tomatoes, chopped
3 tablespoons tomato paste
6 oz (175 g) cheese, grated
14 oz (400 g) wholewheat
  breadcrumbs

1. Cook the pasta shells (or any other small shape such as bows).
2. Sauté onion, garlic and peppers in oil.
3. Add the diced eggplant, bay leaves, salt and herbs.
4. Add zucchini, tomatoes and tomato paste and gently stir it all together.
5. Cover and simmer for about 20 minutes, until sauce thickens.
6. Mix in the cooked pasta shells, and put it all into an oven-proof casserole.
7. Make a gratin topping by combining cheese and bread-crumbs, moistened with a little oil, and spread the mixture over the top. Bake at 350°F (180°C) for 50 minutes.

Serves 6

Lasagna with Zucchini

Made with fresh herbs and vegetables, this lasagna variation makes a wonderful summertime—or anytime—treat.

4 tablespoons butter
4 tablespoons flour
16 fl oz (450 ml or 2 cups) milk
3 cloves garlic, crushed
1 tablespoon chopped thyme
salt and pepper
2 tablespoons olive oil
3 small-medium zucchini, sliced
tomatoes and mushrooms or eggplant
package of lasagna pasta
6-8 oz (175-225 g) Parmesan cheese, grated
buttered bread crumbs

1. Melt butter in a saucepan. Stir in flour, and cook, but do not brown, for 3 to 4 minutes. Remove from heat and whisk in milk all at once. Return to heat, stir and simmer until sauce thickens.
2. Add minced garlic, thyme, salt and pepper.
3. In a frying pan, heat olive oil and sauté sliced zucchini.
4. Place layer of lasagna pasta in large, lightly-oiled baking dish and cover with layer of sauce, layer of zucchini, and other selected vegetables, and a sprinkling of cheese.
5. Repeat layers about six times and top the dish with buttered bread crumbs and more grated Parmesan cheese.
6. Bake uncovered at 350°F (180°C) for 30 minutes.

Serves 8

Zucchini Sausage Bake

Couldn't be easier. Health- or cholesterol-conscious people can use turkey or vegetarian sausages.

1 lb (450 g) zucchini, chopped
1 clove garlic, sliced
1 medium onion, chopped
salt to taste
1 lb (450 g) sausage, cut up
3 eggs, beaten
6 oz (¾ cup or 175 g) Parmesan cheese, grated
15-20 oz (3-4 cups or 425-550 g) cooked rice

1. Mix all the ingredients together and spoon into a shallow baking dish.
2. Bake in a preheated oven at 300°F (150°C) for 1-1½ hours.

Serves 6

Zucchini Tian

A tian is a typical Provencal-style gratin of vegetables. It can make a light main course served with rice or couscous or it can be a zestful side dish served with roast chicken or meat. Preparing it a day ahead can even improve the flavor.

4 tablespoon olive oil
2 medium onions, chopped
2 cloves garlic, chopped
salt and pepper to taste
1 tablespoon shredded fresh basil or oregano
3 medium zucchini, cut into ½ inch (1.2 cm) slices
3 medium tomatoes, thinly sliced
2 oz (½ cup or 50g) grated Parmesan cheese

1. Heat 2 tablespoons of the oil in a frying pan over medium heat. Add onions and garlic and cook, stirring occasionally, until golden, about 10 minutes. Add salt and pepper.
2. Oil the bottom and sides of a 9 x 13 inch (23 x 31 cm) baking dish, and spread the mixture evenly into it. Sprinkle with half the herbs. Over the herbs, place alternating and slightly overlapping slices of zucchini and tomato. Sprinkle with remaining herbs and with the remaining 2 tablespoons of oil.
3. Bake the tian in a preheated oven at 375°F (190°C) until juices are sizzling, about 40-45 minutes. Sprinkle with cheese and bake for another 5 minutes. Remove from oven and allow it to rest for 10 minutes. Serve warm.

Serves 6

Rustic Vegetable Stew

This Mediterranean-style stew, which may be served over rice, calls only for crusty French bread as an accessory.

2 tablespoons olive oil
1 medium onion, chopped
3 garlic cloves, crushed
1 large potato, cut into ½-inch (1.2 cm) cubes
1 medium eggplant, cut into 1-inch (2.5 cm) cubes
large tin (about 28 oz or 700 g) undrained tomatoes
12 fl oz water (1½ cups or 360 ml)
1 teaspoon salt
1 sprig fresh rosemary (or 1 teaspoon dried)
1 medium-large zucchini, sliced
1 green pepper, cut into 1-inch (2.5 cm) pieces
juice of 1 lemon
1 tablespoon chopped fresh dill (or 1 teaspoon dried)
freshly ground black pepper
feta cheese

1. Heat oil in a large pot and sauté the onions and garlic over medium heat until soft and golden. Add potato cubes and eggplant cubes. Mix in the juice from the tomatoes and the water. Add salt and rosemary and bring to a boil. Then reduce heat, and simmer covered for about 10 minutes.
2. Add sliced zucchini and pepper pieces. Continue to simmer, uncovered, for 5 minutes.
3. Add coarsely-chopped tomatoes together with lemon juice and dill, and simmer for another 5 minutes.
4. Add black pepper to taste and remove fresh rosemary sprig.
5. Top with crumbled feta cheese and serve.

Serves 4-6

Chili Sin Carne

This easy-to-prepare recipe for chili offers a beautiful blend of colors and flavors for a superb vegetarian course.

1 medium onion, chopped
½ green pepper, chopped
2 tablespoons olive oil
2-3 cloves garlic, crushed
1 large zucchini, chopped
1 carrot, diced
2 cans (15 oz or 425 g each) kidney beans
2 cans (about 1 lb or 450 g each) tomatoes, peeled and
  chopped
1-2 tablespoons chili powder
¼ teaspoon cumin
¼ teaspoon basil
¼ teaspoon oregano
¼ teaspoon thyme
freshly ground pepper to taste
4 fl oz (½ cup or 120 ml) water

1. In a large pot, sauté onion and green pepper in olive oil over medium heat until onions are soft, about 6-8 minutes.
2. Add garlic, zucchini and carrot and cook over low heat for a further 2 minutes.
3. Rinse and drain kidney beans and add them to the mixture together with tomatoes, seasonings, and water. Stir it all together.
4. Bring mixture to a boil, then reduce heat and simmer for about 35-45 minutes.

Serves 8

Gado-Gado

The richly flavored peanut sauce emanates from Indonesia. It is simple to make and goes well with many dishes. Here it is combined with lightly cooked vegetables to produce a popular Asian dish. As the selection and amount of vegetables may be varied depending on availability and imagination, or number of guests, it could become a popular dish in any kitchen.

2 large squares bean curd
oil for deep frying
zucchini, cut into strips
cauliflower florets
green beans
carrots, sliced diagonally
cabbage, shredded
3 hard-boiled eggs, quartered
boiled potatoes
cucumber, thinly sliced
lettuce, watercress or other salad greens

Peanut Sauce:
2-3 tablespoons peanut or sesame oil
4 shallots, finely chopped
2 cloves garlic, crushed
½ teaspoon chili powder
12 oz (350 g) chunky peanut butter
1 tablespoon lemon juice
1 tablespoon dark soy sauce
1 teaspoon brown sugar
salt to taste

1. Cut the bean curd into large slices and deep fry in hot oil until golden brown. Remove and drain on absorbent paper.
2. Cut boiled eggs into quarters.
3. Prepare freshly cooked vegetables, by boiling separately for 3-4 minutes, so that they may be served warm or at room temperature.
4. Garnish a serving platter with salad greens around the edge. Arrange the bean curd and vegetables in the middle of the platter, placing the quartered eggs, sliced potatoes and cucumber on top. Spoon the peanut sauce over it.
5. For the peanut sauce, heat oil in a pan over low heat. Fry shallots and garlic until they become soft.
6. Add remaining ingredients to the pan, mixing thoroughly. Simmer on low heat for 10-15 minutes, stirring occasionally. Adjust amount of peanut butter if necessary to give a thick pouring consistency. Adjust seasonings.

Fish in Foil

Prepare this one ahead of time for company; when ready, just take foil packets from refrigerator and cook. Couscous would go nicely with this dish. Or rice.

1 small zucchini, thinly sliced
6-8 fresh mushrooms, sliced
1 small red onion, thinly sliced
2 6-oz (175 g) firm fish fillets
2 tablespoons olive oil
juice of 1 lemon
2 fl oz (¼ cup or 60 ml) dry white wine
salt and freshly ground black pepper
1 tablespoon shredded fresh basil (or 1 teaspoon dried)
6 black pitted olives

1. Take 2 sheets of aluminum foil 12 x 24 inches (30 x 60 cm) and fold each sheet in half to form a double thickness.
2. On the center part of each foil square brush a little oil, then arrange on it half of the ingredients: zucchini, mushrooms, fish, onion slices.
3. In a small bowl, combine olive oil, lemon juice, wine, seasonings, and basil and dribble the mixture over each arrangement. Place halved olives on top.
4. Fold the foil into airtight packets.
5. Bake in a preheated oven at 425°F (220°C) for 20-25 minutes.
6. With a spatula, carefully lift the fish and vegetables out of the foil onto individual, warmed serving plates and pour any leftover liquid over each serving.

Serves 2

Indian Prawns with Zucchini

*This recipe produces a lovely Indian dish to give your taste buds
a treat. Serve with basmati rice.*

2 medium-large zucchini (about 1 lb or 450 g)
5 tablespoons oil
6 cloves garlic, crushed
3 oz (75 g) chopped fresh coriander
1 hot green chili
½ teaspoon turmeric
1 ½ teaspoons cumin
¼ teaspoon cayenne
1 teaspoon finely grated fresh ginger
1 small tin of tomatoes
juice of half a lemon
salt, to taste
¾ lb (350 g) peeled prawns (shrimp)

1. Cut zucchini into strips about 2 inches (5 cm.) long.
2. Heat oil in frying pan and put in the zucchini strips and chopped garlic. Sauté for 2-3 minutes.
3. Add coriander, finely chopped green chili, turmeric, cumin, cayenne, ginger, finely chopped tomatoes and their liquid, lemon juice, and salt. Mix ingredients together and bring to a simmer.
4. Stir in the prawns. Cover and simmer for 3 minutes.
5. Uncover, turn heat to medium and boil away liquid to be left with a thick sauce.

Serves 4

Lamb Biryani

You have the option of omitting the lamb if you prefer to make a vegetarian dish. In any case, this simple recipe will produce a tasty Indian treat.

1 large zucchini, thickly sliced
1 carrot, thickly sliced
1 large red onion, cut into wedges
1 red pepper, deseeded and cut into six segments
1 small eggplant, thickly sliced
2 tablespoons olive oil
12 oz (350 g) chopped lamb fillet (optional)
salt and pepper
2 tablespoons mild curry paste
4 oz (125 g) basmati rice
12-16 fl oz (1½-2 cups or 360-450 ml) vegetable stock
2 tablespoons fresh coriander, chopped

1. Toss the vegetables in the oil. Spread out in a roasting pan and sprinkle with salt and freshly ground black pepper. If you opt for a lamb dish, add it to the roasting pan.
2. Cook for 20 minutes in a preheated oven at 375°F (190°C) until vegetables start to turn golden.
3. Stir in the curry paste, rice and stock and cook for another 20-30 minutes or until the liquid is absorbed and rice is tender.
4. Stir in the coriander and serve straight away.

Serves 4

Imam Bayildi

The name of this dish is "The Priest Has Fainted"—ostensibly because the taste was ineffable. This stuffed eggplant recipe, while promising, does not promise to make dinner guests faint.

3 eggplants
4 tablespoons olive oil
1 large onion, chopped
½ large green pepper, chopped
2-3 garlic cloves, crushed
2 small-medium zucchini, chopped
1 lb (450 g) tomatoes, roughly chopped

1 teaspoon sugar
1 teaspoon cinnamon
4 tablespoons raisins
2 tablespoons chopped fresh parsley
½-1 teaspoon salt
freshly ground black pepper

1. Cut eggplants in half lengthwise. Scoop out the flesh leaving a very thin border and chop the insides roughly.
2. Heat oil in a large frying pan and cook the onion, green pepper, and garlic for 5-10 minutes. Add the chopped eggplant and more oil if needed. Continue cooking, stirring occasionally, until the eggplant is soft and lightly browned. Add the zucchini, tomatoes, sugar, cinnamon, raisins, and half the parsley. Cover and cook for a further 5 minutes. Season with salt and pepper. Remove from heat.
3. Brush the inside of the eggplant shells with oil. Spoon the mixture into the shells and sprinkle the remaining parsley over the tops. Place the shells in a shallow baking dish.
4. Bake at 350°F (180°C) for about 40 minutes. Serve warm with white rice and a green salad.

Serves 6

113

Mediterranean Chicken with Zucchini

A wholesome and succulent recipe to add to your healthy cuisine repertoire.

medium-size chicken, skinned and cut into sections
salt and pepper
3 medium zucchini
1 green pepper, cut into strips
1 lb (450 g) fresh mushrooms, cut into thick slices
1 small tin (10 oz or 300 ml) tomatoes, broken up
1 medium onion, chopped
2 garlic cloves, minced
2 teaspoons dried basil
1 bay leaf
Parmesan cheese (optional)

1. Sprinkle chicken with salt and pepper. Arrange pieces on a rack in a pan and bake for 10 minutes in preheated oven at 425°F (210°C). Then lower oven temperature to 350°F (180°C). Remove chicken and rack from pan and pour off any fat. Return chicken to pan.
2. Cut zucchini into 2-inch (5 cm) strips and scatter them over the chicken. Add green pepper strips and mushrooms.
3. In a large bowl, combine tomatoes, onion, garlic, basil, and bay leaf. Stir mixture well and pour over chicken.
4. Cover and bake about 50-60 minutes, or until done.
5. Sprinkle with Parmesan cheese, if desired, and serve.

Serves 4

Veal Cutlets with Zucchini

May also be prepared using chicken breast instead of veal.

6 veal cutlets
1 large egg, slightly beaten
3-4 oz (75-110 g) fine breadcrumbs
2 tablespoons olive oil
1 tin tomatoes, about 1 lb (450 g)
1 teaspoon oregano
½-1 teaspoon salt
freshly ground pepper
3 medium zucchini, sliced

1. Dip the cutlets in beaten egg, then coat in crumbs. Heat oil in pan and brown the cutlets.
2. Add the tomatoes, broken up, the oregano, salt, and a few grinds of pepper. Cover pan and simmer for 30 minutes.
3. Add sliced zucchini and cook for another 15-20 minutes.

Serves 6

Chinese Ground Beef with Zucchini and Tomatoes

*Chicken or shrimp could be substituted for the ground beef.
Serve with rice, of course.*

½ lb (225 g) ground (minced) beef
1 medium onion, sliced
3 tablespoons soy sauce
2 cloves of garlic, minced
salt and pepper, to taste
3 tablespoons oil
2 small zucchini, sliced diagonally
4 fl oz (½ cup or 120 ml) water
2 tomatoes, cut into wedges
½ teaspoon brown sugar
1 tablespoon cornstarch dissolved in 2 oz (¼ cup or 60 ml)
   water

1. Mix ground beef, onion, soy sauce, garlic, and salt and pepper together.
2. Heat oil in wok or frying pan and stir fry ground beef mixture until browned, about 2-3 minutes.
3. Stir in zucchini and water. Cover pan and cook for five minutes, stirring two or three times. Add more water, if needed.
4. Add tomatoes and sugar. Cover and continue to cook for a further 2-3 minutes.
5. Mix together cornstarch and water and add the solution to the pan, stirring to thicken.

Serves 2-4

116

Accompaniments

Basic Zucchini with Fresh Herbs

This simple dish is especially good early in the season, when zucchini are young and tender and have the best flavor.

1½ lbs (700 g) young zucchini, sliced
1 oz (25 g) butter
1 tablespoon finely chopped fresh parsley
1 tablespoon finely chopped fresh chives
salt and freshly ground black pepper

1. Steam sliced zucchini for about 5 minutes until tender but not soggy.
2. Drain and add butter, herbs, and seasonings.

Serves 4-6

Sautéed Zucchini in Olive Oil

A quick and easy way to produce a good zucchini dish.

1 lb (450 g) small zucchini
2 fluid oz (50 ml) olive oil
chopped parsley or basil leaves
salt and pepper

1. Cut unpeeled zucchini into ½ inch (1.2 cm) slices.
2. Sauté the slices in the olive oil in a large frying pan about 5-6 minutes until they are tender and nicely browned on each side.
3. Season with salt and pepper. Spoon into a serving dish and sprinkle with chopped parsley or basil.

Serves 4

Sautéed Zucchini with Herbs

Seasoned with herbs, this version of sauté cooking makes another delicious accompanying vegetable.

1½ lbs (700 g) zucchini
4 tablespoons olive oil
salt and pepper, to taste
2 tablespoons butter
2 garlic cloves, chopped
1 tablespoon chopped parsley
1 tablespoon chopped chives
1 tablespoon chopped dill
1 tablespoon chopped tarragon
1 tablespoon chopped fresh basil

1. Cut unpeeled zucchini into very thin slices.
2. Add zucchini to oil that has been heated in a frying pan. Sprinkle with salt and pepper and cook over high heat, stirring gently and turning the slices over, until golden— about 5-6 minutes.
3. Add butter to the pan and, when melted, add garlic and herbs. Mix gently and serve hot.

Serves 4-6

Sautéed Zucchini with Yogurt

This could hardly be easier. Or quicker.

2 tablespoons butter
3 medium zucchini
1 medium onion, chopped
salt and freshly ground black pepper to taste
2 tablespoons chopped herbs (parsley or chives)
grated cheese (optional)
1 tablespoon yogurt

1. Cut zucchini into small cubes and sauté in butter with a chopped onion until tender. Add salt and grind in pepper to taste.
2. Sprinkle with herbs. Add grated cheese, if desired.
3. Stir in the yogurt and serve.

Serves 4-6

121

Turkish Zucchini with Yogurt

Unbelievably easy—as well as delicious.

4 small-medium zucchini
olive oil
salt and pepper
pinch of nutmeg
2 tablespoons chopped fresh herbs (parsley, basil, or mint)
8 tablespoons yogurt

1. Cut each zucchini lengthwise into 4 long slices of about ½ inch (1.2 cm) thick.
2. Fry the slices in hot oil quickly, until brown, turning once.
3. Drain on paper towels and remove to serving dish.
4. Season with salt and pepper, nutmeg and herbs.
5. Spoon yogurt over and serve hot.

Serves 4

Zucchini with Tomatoes and Garlic

This is an ideal vegetable dish to serve with a main course.

6 medium zucchini
2 tablespoons butter or olive oil
2-3 cloves garlic, minced
2 tomatoes, peeled and diced
salt and pepper
2 tablespoons parsley, chopped

1. Cut unpeeled zucchini into thick rounds.
2. Heat butter or oil in a saucepan and cook garlic on low heat. Stir in the tomatoes. Add zucchini and season with salt and freshly ground pepper.
3. Cover and continue cooking on low heat for about 10-15 minutes or until zucchini is tender. Stir occasionally and add a little water if needed.
4. Sprinkle with parsley and serve.

Serves 4-6

Stuffed Zucchini

Health-conscious people can substitute curd or low-fat cheese and wholemeal breadcrumbs in this simple-to-make dish.

4 medium-large zucchini, unpeeled
4 oz (110 g) white breadcrumbs
8 oz (225 g) cream cheese (or low-fat white cheese)
4 tablespoons flaked almonds
rind and juice of ½ lemon
salt and freshly ground black pepper

1. Boil zucchini for 4-5 minutes. Cool and slice them in half lengthwise. Remove center pulp and set aside. Arrange zucchini in a buttered baking dish.
2. In a small bowl, mix together the breadcrumbs, cheese, almonds, lemon juice and rind (to taste), and mashed zucchini centers. Add salt and pepper and blend.
3. Fill the zucchini with this mixture and bake in oven preheated to 350°F (180°C) for 40-45 minutes.

Serves 4

Zucchini with Chick Pea Stuffing

This is yet another way to stuff zucchini. It can also be chilled and served in Middle Eastern style with yogurt.

4 medium-large zucchini
½ oz (15 g) butter
1 onion, chopped
2 garlic cloves, crushed
8-10 mushrooms, sliced
about 4 oz (110 g) chickpeas
1-2 teaspoons ground coriander
2 tablespoons lemon juice
2 tablespoons chopped parsley
salt and freshly ground black pepper, to taste

1. Cut unpeeled zucchini in half lengthwise. Remove center pulp, chop, and set aside. Arrange courgette shells in a buttered baking dish.
2. Melt the butter in a pan, and sauté the onion and garlic for 5 minutes, then add the chopped zucchini centers and the sliced mushrooms and cook for another 5 minutes.
3. Add drained chickpeas, ground coriander, lemon juice, parsley, and salt and pepper. Blend well and fill the zucchini shells with the mixture.
4. Bake in oven preheated to 350°F (180°C) about 30 minutes, or until zucchini are tender.

Serves 4

Zucchini with Parmesan Cheese

Walnuts and cheese contribute to an interesting blend of flavors.

8 small zucchini
butter
2 garlic cloves, minced
finely chopped parsley
grated Parmesan cheese
2 tablespoons chopped walnuts
salt and freshly ground black pepper

1. Cut zucchini in half lengthwise. Dot each open half with butter, garlic, parsley, cheese, and chopped walnuts. Sprinkle with salt and pepper.
2. Grill for a few minutes, allowing the top to cook while the zucchini remain crisp and partially uncooked.

Serves 4

Zucchini with Apricots

This is a delightful Middle-Eastern dish.

6 small zucchini (about 2 lbs or nearly 1 kg), cut into ¼-inch (1.6 cm) rounds
3 tablespoons olive oil
8 oz (225 g) small dried apricots
8 fl oz (1 cup or 240 ml) water
2 tablespoons lemon juice
1 tablespoon brown sugar
salt and pepper

1. Boil the water in a small saucepan and add apricots. Cover and simmer about 15 minutes until apricots are tender. Add sugar and lemon juice. Set aside.
2. Heat oil in a pan and sauté the zucchini over medium heat for 5 minutes, stirring frequently. Add salt and pepper.
3. Pour the apricot mixture, undrained, over the zucchini. Cook, covered, about 5 minutes until the zucchini are tender but still crisp.
4. If a thicker sauce is desired, stir a tablespoon of cornstarch with 2 tablespoons of water and add to pan, cooking for a minute or two until the sauce thickens.

8 servings

127

Sweet and Sour Zucchini

*With an intriguing hint of cinnamon, this recipe is good served
with grilled meat, roast chicken, or turkey.*

**2 lbs (1 kg) zucchini
2 tablespoons olive oil
salt and freshly ground black pepper
½ teaspoon cinnamon
4 tablespoons white wine vinegar
1 tablespoon sugar
2 tablespoons water**

1. Sauté sliced, unpeeled zucchini gently in olive oil until nearly tender, about 8-10 minutes.
2. Season with salt and black pepper and cinnamon. Add wine vinegar and sugar.
3. Stir gently, turning zucchini slices over until the liquid is reduced to a smaller amount and the flavors are absorbed by the zucchini, making certain not to overcook.

Serves 4-6

Sicilian Style Sweet and Sour Zucchini

The southern Italy version of sweet and sour zucchini.

2 lbs (1 kg) zucchini
2 large cloves garlic, crushed
3 tablespoons olive oil
3 tablespoons red wine vinegar
2 tablespoons water
1 oz (25 g) raisins or sultanas
1 oz (25 g) pine kernels
8 anchovy fillets
salt and freshly ground black pepper

1. Heat the oil in a large frying pan and sauté garlic. Add zucchini, cut into strips 2-3 inches (5-8 cm) long, and stir gently until they turn golden.
2. Add vinegar and water. Cover and simmer for 10-12 minutes.
3. Add raisins, pine kernels, and anchovies (rinsed of any salt or oil and chopped) and cook uncovered, until the liquid is reduced.
4. Add salt and pepper and stir to steep zucchini in the flavors of the sauce.

Serves 4-6

Zucchini Strips with Mint

This unusual way of preparing zucchini takes only about ten minutes. It makes a good accompaniment to many main courses, especially lamb.

4 small zucchini (1 lb or 450 g), peeled
1 tablespoon olive oil
2 garlic cloves, minced
pinch of salt
2 tablespoons chopped fresh mint

1. Slice the zucchini into very thin long strips with a potato peeler.
2. In a frying pan, sauté garlic in oil over medium heat for a minute or two.
3. Raise heat to high and add zucchini strips and salt. Cook and stir until zucchini wilts—about 2 minutes.
4. Remove from heat and stir in mint.

Serves 4

Zucchini and Carrots à la Menthe

Colorful and easy.

3 carrots, sliced into ¼ inch (less than 1 cm) rounds
2 medium zucchini, sliced into ¼ inch (less than 1 cm)
**   rounds**
2 tablespoons butter
salt and freshly ground pepper
2 teaspoons fresh mint, chopped

1. Heat butter in a heavy frying pan and cook the sliced carrots in it, covered, for about 4-5 minutes.
2. Add sliced zucchini. Sprinkle with salt and pepper to taste. Cover and cook another 4-5 minutes, stirring occasionally, until vegetables are tender. Sprinkle with mint.

4 servings

Dijon Carrots and Zucchini

This fatless recipe blends mustard and other ingredients and carrots to give the zucchini a sweet and savory flavor.

2-3 medium zucchini cut into 2-inch (5 cm) sticks
2 medium-large carrots cut into 2-inch (5 cm) sticks
2 tablespoons chicken broth
1 teaspoon apple cider vinegar
1 teaspoon honey
1½ teaspoons Dijon mustard
salt and pepper to taste

1. Cut zucchini into 2-inch (5 cm) sticks and set aside.
2. Cut carrots into 2-inch (5 cm) sticks and cook them in the broth in a covered saucepan over medium heat for 10 minutes.
3. Add zucchini and cook for another 5 minutes or until vegetables are tender, adding more broth if necessary.
4. Mix vinegar, honey and mustard together and stir the mixture into the vegetables. Add salt and pepper.
5. Cook for a few more minutes until liquid evaporates.

4-6 servings

Poor Person's Zucchini

There is nothing poor about this healthy regional dish which derives its name from the fact that in southern Italy (Apulia) the ingredients would be inexpensive or readily available from the garden.

8 small-medium zucchini
6 tablespoons olive oil
1 bunch of fresh mint, coarsely chopped
8 tablespoons red wine vinegar
2-3 large cloves garlic, chopped
pinch of salt (optional)

1. Slice the zucchini lengthwise into thin strips.
2. Heat the oil, and fry zucchini and chopped garlic for about 4-5 minutes, turning the strips over, until golden. Drain on paper towels.
3. Arrange in layers in a serving dish or casserole and sprinkle with half the mint.
4. Measure wine vinegar into a pan, adding salt (if desired) and remaining mint. Bring to the boil, then simmer for about 5 minutes. Pour the hot marinade all over the zucchini.
5. Allow to cool. Serve slightly chilled.

Serves 6-8

Lemon Zucchini

Another simple recipe that is simply good.

4 small zucchini
2 tablespoons butter
2 tablespoons lemon juice
½ teaspoon grated lemon rind
salt and pepper to taste
chopped parsley

1. Cut zucchini into ¼-inch (.6 cm) slices. Cook uncovered in boiling water for 3-4 minutes, or steam. Drain.
2. Heat butter, lemon juice and lemon rind in a small saucepan, stirring until butter is melted. Season with salt and pepper. Pour over the zucchini. Garnish with parsley.

4 servings

Zucchini with Oil and Lemon

Another way to use lemon with zucchini.

3 large zucchini
3 tablespoons olive oil
salt and pepper
juice of half a lemon

1. Cut zucchini into quarters, then into two-inch (5 cm) lengths.
2. Heat oil in a frying pan and add zucchini; sprinkle with salt and pepper to taste. Cook until they turn golden.
3. Add lemon juice. Cover and cook about 3 minutes, until crisp.

4 servings

Grated Zucchini with Lemon Juice

Lemon again, but with a very different effect.

2 large zucchini (about 1 lb or 500 g)
juice of 1 lemon
salt and pepper, to taste
1 teaspoon fresh tarragon or basil
2 oz (50 g) butter

1. Grate zucchini finely and mix with fresh lemon juice.
2. Add salt and pepper and tarragon or basil. Refrigerate for at least 5 hours.
3. When ready to serve, sauté the mixture in heated butter for about 4 minutes.

Serves 4-6

Zucchini à l'Orange

This may be prepared in advance and refrigerated. When ready to serve, simmer until heated through.

2 lbs (nearly 1 kg) zucchini, sliced into rounds
3 oz (80 g) butter
salt and pepper
2 tablespoons orange juice
1 tablespoon grated orange rind

1. Sauté thinly-sliced zucchini in butter until just tender.
2. Season with salt and pepper
3. Remove from heat. Add orange juice and orange rind and mix together.

Serves 6

Zucchini Fans

Cutting zucchini into fan shapes makes such an attractive presentation that people will think you put in a lot more effort than this surprisingly easy—as well as tasty—recipe actually calls for.

4 small zucchinis (about 4-5 oz or 125 g each)
salt and pepper
a little flour
2 tablespoons butter

1. Trim zucchini and slice them lengthwise into a fan shape, cutting up to ¾ inch (2 cm) of the stalk end, to hold the slices together.
2. Open out the fan. Sprinkle with salt and pepper. Dip the zucchini fans into flour and shake off any excess.
3. Heat butter in a large skillet and fry for 5 minutes on each side. Add more butter if needed.

Serves 4

Marrow in Tomato and Coriander Sauce

Next time you have an overgrown zucchini, try cooking it in this tomato sauce recipe for a spicy and delicious result.

1 marrow (about 1½-2 lbs or 700-900 g)
1 onion, chopped
2 tablespoons olive oil
2 tablespoons tomato paste
2 teaspoons coriander seeds, coarsely crushed
1 teaspoon green peppercorns
salt and freshly ground black pepper
½ teaspoon sugar (optional)

1. Peel marrow and cut into small cubes.
2. Sauté onion in oil in a pan for 5 minutes.
3. Add marrow, tomato paste, coriander, green peppercorns, salt and pepper. Mix.
4. Cover and simmer gently for about 15 minutes until marrow is nearly tender. Then boil uncovered for 5-10 minutes until liquid has evaporated.
5. Adjust seasonings and add sugar, if needed.

Serves 4

Spicy Ginger Marrow

This savory recipe can also be made with smaller zucchini.

1 marrow, about 1½-2 lbs (700-900 g)
1 medium onion, chopped
2 tablespoons olive oil
1-2 teaspoons ground ginger
2 oz (50 g) stem ginger, chopped
salt and pepper
fresh parsley, chopped

1. Peel marrow and cut into small cubes. It is not necessary to remove seeds if tender.
2. Heat oil in a pan and sauté onion for 5 minutes. Add marrow together with ground and chopped ginger.
3. Cook gently in covered pan until marrow is nearly tender, about 15 minutes.
4. Then uncover and allow to boil for 5-10 minutes until liquid has evaporated.
5. Season with salt and pepper to taste and sprinkle with chopped parsley before serving.

Serves 4

Mexican Zucchini and Corn in Tomato Sauce

*Zucchini or **calabacitas** are basic to a Mexican diet and are often added to sauces. This excellent side dish uses a method of charring and skinning vegetables, popular in Mexico, that imparts a sweet and smoky flavor.*

4 ripe tomatoes, charred and peeled
½ green chili, charred
1 clove garlic, charred
½ onion, charred
2 teaspoons oil
4 fl oz (120 ml) water
4 zucchini, cubed
4 oz (110 g) fresh or frozen corn kernels
¼ teaspoon salt
pinch of freshly ground black pepper

1. Skin tomatoes, chili, garlic and onion by charring them under the grill or in a hot and heavy frying pan. Turn frequently until black and blistered, and peel when cool enough to handle.
2. Purée the vegetables in a blender or food processor.
3. Heat the oil in a saucepan and cook the purée for 3 minutes, stirring continually.
4. Add the water, zucchini, corn, salt and pepper, and simmer for about 10 minutes. Serve hot.

Serves 4

Puebla Style Zucchini

*This adaptation of a Mexican recipe for **calabacitas**, or
zucchini, substitutes green peppers for **poblano**, a local green
pepper used in **mole poblano**, the famous dish of the state of
Puebla. Sweet green peppers will also yield excellent results for
this unusual vegetable dish that goes well with any plain meat,
poultry, or fish. You can also vary it by topping with slices of
cheese such as Spanish **queso blanco** or mild Cheddar to make
an attractive vegetarian lunch dish.*

3 sweet green peppers, toasted, peeled, and seeded
1 medium onion, chopped
1 clove garlic, chopped
3 tablespoons vegetable oil
1 lb (450 g) small zucchini, cut into ½ inch (1.2 cm) cubes
4 fl oz (120 ml) water
salt and pepper
5 tablespoons heavy cream

1. Chop the toasted, peeled, and seeded peppers coarsely and
    purée them in a food processor with the onion and garlic.
2. Heat the oil in a saucepan and sauté the purée, stirring
    constantly for about 3-4 minutes. Add the zucchini, and
    season to taste with salt and pepper.
3. Add the water. Cover and simmer until the zucchini are
    tender, about 20 minutes. Add more water, if needed. (There
    should be just enough liquid to cook the zucchini.)
4. Stir in the cream and simmer, uncovered, just long enough
    to heat it through.

Serves 4-6

Zucchini Rice

Any leftovers are also delicious served cold, as a salad. It may also be frozen.

2 tablespoons olive oil
2 onions, chopped
2 large garlic cloves, crushed
1 large red pepper, chopped
1½ lbs (700 g) zucchini, sliced
6 oz (175 g) brown rice
14 oz (400 g) tin tomatoes
salt and freshly ground black pepper
2 tablespoons chopped parsley

1. Sauté the onions and garlic in the oil for 5 minutes, until golden. Add pepper and cook for another 3-4 minutes.
2. Add the rice and zucchini, stirring to coat them with oil.
3. Add the tomatoes and salt and pepper.
4. Bring to a boil, then reduce heat. Cover and simmer gently over low heat for 40 minutes. There should be enough liquid from the vegetables for cooking the rice. Otherwise, add water.
5. Remove pan from heat, stir mixture, and allow to stand, covered, for about 10 minutes.
6. Adjust seasonings. Sprinkle with parsley and serve.

Serves 6

Farfalle with Zucchini, Peas, and Mint

Farfalle are pasta in the shape of bow ties or butterflies. Of course, you can use other shapes such as ribbons or fettuccine.

8-12 oz (225-350 g) farfalle
1 oz (25 g) butter
1 tablespoon olive oil
1 lb (450 g) zucchini, thinly sliced
6 oz (175 g) shelled peas
2 tablespoons chopped mint
salt and freshly ground black pepper
grated Parmesan cheese

1. Cook pasta in boiling water until just tender. Drain.
2. Meanwhile, cook the zucchini and peas in melted butter and oil over low heat for about 6-8 minutes.
3. Turn zucchini and peas, together with pan juices, into a hot serving dish. Add hot, drained pasta and chopped mint. Gently mix it all together, adding salt and a few grinds of pepper.
4. Sprinkle with grated Parmesan cheese and serve.

Serves 4-6

Baked Zucchini with Goat Cheese

Other cheeses such as cheddar or mozzarella may be substituted.

8 small zucchini, unpeeled
2 tablespoons olive oil
3-4 oz (about 80-110 g) goat cheese
fresh mint, finely chopped
freshly ground black pepper

1. Cut a thin slit lengthwise in each courgette.
2. Insert strips of goat cheese into slits. Add mint and a few grinds of pepper. Sprinkle with 1 tablespoon of the oil.
3. Wrap each zucchini in a rectangle of aluminum foil that has been brushed with the remaining oil.
4. Bake in preheated oven at 350°F (180°C) for about 20-25 minutes.

Serves 4

Zucchini and Cheese Gratin

Pungent feta cheese takes away any blandness attributed to zucchini, but you may substitute for it an equal mixture of cottage cheese and grated Parmesan.

3 large zucchini
1 lb (450 g) feta cheese
3 eggs, lightly beaten
salt and pepper to taste
pinch of nutmeg
4-5 sprigs of fresh mint or 3 teaspoons dried mint

1. Cut zucchini into thick slices. Boil for a few minutes, until just tender but still crisp, and drain. Arrange them closely together in a lightly-greased shallow baking dish.
2. Mash the feta with a fork and add the rest of the ingredients. Stir well and spoon the mixture over the zucchini.
3. Bake in a preheated 350°F (180°C) oven for about 30 minutes, until the top is lightly browned.
4. Serve hot or cold. May be served with yogurt.

Serves 6-8

Grilled Garlic Zucchini

Zucchini is an excellent vegetable choice for grilling on your outdoor barbecue. Mix green and yellow ones, if you have them, for an even more colorful effect.

6 medium-large zucchini, cut in half lengthwise
2 cloves garlic, crushed
1 tablespoon olive oil
juice of half a lemon
1 ½ teaspoons basil
salt and pepper

1. Mix together garlic, oil, lemon juice, and seasonings. Brush cut surfaces of zucchini with half of this garlic mixture.
2. Place on preheated grill, cut side down, and grill for 4 minutes.
3. Turn and brush with remaining garlic mixture and cook for another 4 minutes or until tender.

6 servings

Baked Zucchini Sticks

This attractive and delicious vegetable recipe can be served topped with tomato sauce.

1 lb (450 g) zucchini
3 tablespoons wheat germ
¼ teaspoon garlic powder
½ teaspoon paprika
1 teaspoon oregano
salt and pepper to taste

1. Cut 2 large unpeeled zucchini lengthwise into eighths—or 4 small zucchini lengthwise into quarters.
2. Combine remaining ingredients in a small bowl. Mix well and spread onto a plate.
3. Press cut sides of zucchini into the mixture so that the crumbs stick.
4. Arrange zucchini, cut sides up, on a lightly oiled baking sheet. Any leftover crumbs can be sprinkled over the top.
5. Bake in preheated 400° F (200°C) oven for 15 minutes, until tender but still crisp.

4 servings

Baked Zucchini with Tomatoes

Makes a colorful presentation.

2 medium zucchini
4 medium tomatoes
1 green pepper, chopped
l medium onion, chopped
salt and pepper to taste
3-4 tablespoons olive oil

1. Cut zucchini and tomatoes into slices. Arrange them in a lightly-buttered baking dish, alternating and slightly over-lapping the zucchini and tomato slices.
2. Scatter green pepper, onion, salt and pepper over the top and sprinkle with oil.
3. Bake in hot oven at 400°F (200°C) for about 20-25 minutes.

Serves 2-4

Roasted Summer Vegetables

Baked vegetables are easy and delicious, and this method prevents them from drying out. Substitutions or additions such as carrots or strips of red pepper can yield an even greater color medley for this attractive dish which goes well with roast chicken or grilled meat or fish.

6 baby zucchini
6 baby eggplants
1 lb (450 g) green beans
6 new potatoes
4 fl oz (½ cup or 120 ml) olive oil
salt

1. Arrange vegetables close together to fill a shallow baking dish in a single layer.
2. Sprinkle with olive oil and salt.
3. Bake in oven preheated to 375°F (190°C) until brown and wilted. Since cooking times vary for different vegetables, remove them as they become tender—about 30 minutes for zucchini and eggplant, perhaps an hour for potatoes—and arrange them on a serving plate.
4. Serve at room temperature for maximum flavor.

6 servings

Cheese-Stuffed Zucchini

Another way to appreciate stuffed zucchini as an accompanying vegetable.

6 small zucchini
2 oz (50 g) grated Parmesan cheese
1 egg
3 oz (80 g) fine breadcrumbs
salt and pepper to taste
2 tomatoes, coarsely chopped

1. Slice each zucchini in half lengthwise and parboil them. Remove center pulp and set aside.
2. Mix together the cheese, egg, and breadcrumbs. Season with salt and pepper. Use this mixture to fill each zucchini half.
3. Place the pulp and tomato pieces in a baking dish, and arrange the filled zucchini halves on top.
4. Cover and cook in a low oven, 325°F (160°C) for 40-45 minutes.

Serves 6

Vermouth Zucchini with Onions

If you have no vermouth, use dry sherry instead.

6 tablespoons dry vermouth
6 small-medium zucchini, thinly sliced
l large onion, chopped
1 tablespoon fresh thyme (or 1 teaspoon dried)
salt
freshly ground black pepper

1. In a large frying pan, heat 3 tablespoons of vermouth.
2. Add all the other ingredients and cook over medium heat for about 7 minutes, stirring occasionally. Add the remaining vermouth when mixture starts becoming dry. Cover and cook about 15 minutes, until zucchini is tender but still crisp.
3. Taste for seasonings and serve.

4-6 servings

Curried Zucchini

If you like curry, here's an easy recipe for your repertory. Moreover, you can use it for any vegetable.

3 tablespoons olive oil
1-2 cloves garlic, minced
1 medium onion, chopped
salt and pepper to taste
2 teaspoons curry powder
pinch of red or cayenne pepper (optional)
3 medium zucchini, sliced
2 tomatoes, cut into small pieces

1. In a large frying pan, sauté garlic and onion in olive oil until soft.
2. Add salt and pepper, curry powder—and red pepper, if desired. Mix well.
3. Add the zucchini and cook until tender, about 8-10 minutes.
4. Stir in tomatoes, adjust seasonings, and serve.

Serves 4-6

Southwestern Zucchini with Corn and Green Chilies

Since chilies, basic to the cooking style of the American Southwest, vary greatly in both size and taste, check intensity to make sure the type you use is not too hot for your taste.

2 oz (¼ cup or 50 g) butter
1 tablespoon olive oil
1 medium onion, chopped
4 oz (½ cup or 100 g) chopped fresh green chilies
4 small-medium zucchini, cut into ½-inch (1.2 cm) slices
12-16 oz (1½-2 cups or 350-450 g) fresh (or frozen) corn
   kernels
¼ teaspoon dried oregano
¼ teaspoon cumin
½ teaspoon salt
4 fl oz (½ cup or 120 ml) chicken stock

1. In a frying pan, heat butter and olive oil. Sauté onion and green chili for about 3 minutes.
2. Add zucchini, corn (cut from about 4 ears), oregano, cumin, and salt. Mix well.
3. Add stock. Cover and simmer for about 5 minutes, until zucchini is tender and crisp.

Serves 6

Bread and Cake

Zucchini Bread

As this recipe makes two loaves, keep one in the freezer for emergency use. You can also store chopped zucchini in measured quantities in the freezer, ready for baking in those off-season months when zucchini is not available from your garden.

3 eggs, beaten
4 oz (½ cup or 110 g) granulated sugar
5 oz (140 g) brown sugar
4 fl oz (½ cup or 120 ml) sunflower oil
3 teaspoons maple flavoring
2 zucchini, coarsely chopped (2 cups, about 1 lb or 450 g)
2 teaspoons baking soda (bicarbonate of soda)
½ teaspoon baking powder
½ teaspoon salt
4 oz (½ cup or 110 g) wheat germ
20 oz (2½ cups or 550 g) flour
4 oz (½ cup or 110 g) walnuts, chopped
4-6 tablespoons sesame seeds

1. Beat eggs. Add sugars, oil and maple flavoring, and beat all together until thick and foamy. Stir in zucchini.
2. Add baking soda, baking powder, salt, wheat germ and flour. Mix well. Blend in the walnuts.
3. Turn batter into two greased 9 x 5 inch (23 x 13 cm) loaf pans. Sprinkle sesame seeds over tops.
4. Bake in preheated oven at 350°F (180°C) for 45-55 minutes or until a toothpick inserted into center comes out clean.

Yields 2 loaves, 12 slices each

Zucchini Spice Bread

*Here's another good cake for your afternoon tea repertory, or
for any occasion.*

8 oz (1 cup or 225 g) white flour
8 oz (2 cup or 225 g) whole
  wheat flour
¼ teaspoon salt
2½ teaspoons baking powder
¼ teaspoon nutmeg
½ teaspoon allspice
½ teaspoon cinnamon
½ teaspoon ginger
4 fl oz (½ cup or 120 ml) honey

6 tablespoons melted butter
2 eggs
½ teaspoon vanilla
2 zucchini, coarsely grated
  (2 cups, about 1 lb or
  450 g)
4 oz (½ cup or 110 g)
  chopped nuts
4 oz (½ cup or 110 g)
  raisins (optional)

1. Sift flours into a bowl together with salt, baking powder, nutmeg, allspice, cinnamon, ginger, and set aside.
2. In a large bowl, beat the honey at high speed until it is opaque. Beat in the butter, eggs, and vanilla, continuing to beat for a few more minutes.
3. Add dry ingredients to the mixture alternately with the zucchini, beginning and ending with the dry ingredients. Blend after each addition.
4. Stir in nuts and raisins.
5. Pour into a buttered, medium-size loaf pan about 10 x 6 inches (25 x 15 cm).
6. Bake 30-35 minutes in preheated oven at 350°F (180°C) until toothpick inserted into center comes out clean.

Makes 1 loaf, about 16 slices

Zucchini Pineapple Bread

This bread is more like cake and excellent served at afternoon tea.

3 eggs
8 fl oz (1 cup or 240 ml) vegetable oil
16 oz (2 cups or 450g) sugar (or less)
1 teaspoon vanilla
2 unpeeled medium zucchini, (about 1 lb or 450 g) shredded
1 can crushed pineapple, drained (about 20 oz or 550 g)
1 lb (3 cups or 450 g) flour
2 teaspoons baking soda (bicarbonate of soda)
½ teaspoon baking powder
1½ teaspoons cinnamon
¾ teaspoon nutmeg
1 teaspoon salt
8 oz (225 g) finely chopped walnuts
8 oz (225 g) raisins

1. Combine eggs, vegetable oil, sugar, and vanilla in a large bowl and beat until thick and foamy.
2. Mix in zucchini and drained pineapple.
3. Add sifted flour and the rest of the ingredients. Blend well.
4. Spoon batter into two greased 9 x 5 inch (23 x 13 cm) loaf pans. Bake in preheated oven at 350°F (180°C) 55 to 60 minutes or until toothpick inserted in the center comes out clean.

Yield: 2 loaves

Zucchini Muffins

This is a healthy muffin that is low in cholesterol—and delicious.

5 oz (1 cup or 140 g) whole wheat flour
5 oz (1 cup or 140 g) white flour
2 teaspoons baking soda (bicarbonate of soda)
¼ teaspoon baking powder
1 tablespoon cinnamon
1 egg
4 fl oz (½ cup or 120 ml) sunflower oil
6 oz (175 g) sugar (or less)
4 oz (100 g) nonfat dry milk
3 zucchini, grated (2½ cups or about 1½ lbs or 550 g)
2 teaspoons vanilla
1 tablespoon lemon juice
4 oz (½ cup or 110 g) raisins
3 oz (80 g) chopped walnuts

1. Mix together flours, baking soda, baking powder and cinnamon. Set aside.
2. In another bowl beat together egg, oil, and sugar. Add powdered milk, grated zucchini, vanilla and lemon juice and beat thoroughly.
3. Add flour mixture and mix until smooth.
4. Stir in raisins and walnuts.
5. Spoon into greased muffin cups, two-thirds full. Bake in preheated oven at 350°C (180°F) for 15-20 minutes.

Makes 2 dozen muffins

Carrot and Zucchini Cake

The grated carrot-zucchini combination is the basis for an
excellent cake.

8 oz (225 g) flour
2 teaspoons baking powder
1 teaspoon baking soda
1 teaspoon salt
8 oz (225 g) sugar
1 oz (25 g) pine nuts
1 oz (25 g) sultanas or raisins
2 mashed ripe bananas
3 eggs, beaten
8 oz (225 g) mixed carrots and
  zucchini, grated
5 fl oz (150 ml) sunflower oil

Frosting:
5 oz (140 g) cream cheese
4 oz (110 g) softened butter
½ teaspoon vanilla
8 oz (225 g) icing sugar

1. Sift flour into a large bowl and add baking powder, baking soda, and salt. Mix in sugar, pine nuts and sultanas.
2. Add mashed bananas and beaten eggs. Stir in the grated carrots and zucchini. Add the oil and beat thoroughly for a minute to obtain a thick and slightly lumpy mixture.
3. Spoon the batter into a greased 9-inch (23 cm) cake tin, preferably spring form, and bake in preheated oven at 350°F (180°C) for 50-60 minutes, or until a toothpick inserted into the center comes out clean. Let stand for a few minutes before removing cake from the tin.
4. To make the frosting, beat cream cheese, butter and vanilla until smooth. Gradually add sugar, beating after each addition. Allow icing to stand for a while until it is of right consistency to spread.

Wholemeal Zucchini and Raisin Cake

*Good eaten plain, this moist cake may also be spread with
cream cheese frosting.*

7 oz. (200 g.) wholemeal flour
1 teaspoon baking soda (bicarbonate of soda)
2 teaspoons baking powder
1 teaspoon salt
1 teaspoon ground ginger
8 oz (1 cup or 225 g) brown sugar
4 oz. (½ cup or 110 g) raisins
1 medium zucchini (8 oz or 225 g), grated
2 oz (50 g) grated carrot
7 oz (200 g) crushed pineapple, drained
8 fl oz (1 cup or 240 ml) plain yogurt
3 large eggs, beaten
5 fl oz (150 ml) sunflower oil

1. Put flour, baking soda, baking powder, salt, ginger, sugar
   and raisins in a large mixing bowl. Stir in the grated
   zucchini and carrots and the drained pineapple.
2. Add the yogurt, eggs, and oil.
3. Beat thoroughly for 1 minute to yield a thick batter.
4. Scrape the batter into a greased 9-inch (23 cm) round cake
   tin and bake in preheated 350°F (180°C) oven for 1 hour,
   until a toothpick inserted into the center comes out clean.
   Cool slightly before turning out.

Chocolate Zucchini Layer Cake

Perhaps an unlikely combination, but you're in for a yummy surprise. So are friends, who will never guess the secret ingredient.

4 oz (110 g) butter
6 tablespoons sugar
2 eggs
3 oz (80 g) baking chocolate
2 tablespoons clear honey
5 oz (1 cup or 140 g) flour
2 tablespoons unsweetened cocoa
1½ teaspoons baking powder
4 fl oz (½ cup or 140 ml) milk
1 teaspoon vanilla
1 medium courgette, grated

Frosting:
2 oz (50 g) plain chocolate
3 tablespoons water
2 tablespoons butter
8 oz (225 g) confectioner's (icing) sugar, sifted

1. Cream together butter and sugar until light and fluffy. Beat in the eggs.
2. Stir chocolate and honey in a small bowl over a pan of hot water until the chocolate has melted. Cool. Then beat the chocolate mixture into the butter, sugar, and eggs.
3. Sift together flour, cocoa, and baking powder. Stir in the flour mixture, a little at a time, alternating with milk and vanilla.

4. Stir in grated zucchini and mix well.
5. Pour the mixture into two greased 7 ½ inch (18-19 cm) cake tins.
6. Bake in preheated oven at 350°F (180°C) oven for about 30-35 minutes, until a toothpick inserted in the center comes out clean.
7. For frosting, melt the chocolate and water in a small saucepan over low heat. Remove from heat and stir in butter until it melts. Beat in the sugar. Spread over cake.

Chocolate Zucchini Cake

Although the zucchini is a subtle ingredient in this recipe, it yields a moist and flavorful cake.

4 oz (110 g) butter
4 fl oz (½ cup or 120 ml) sunflower oil
4 oz (½ cup or 110 g) granulated sugar
5 oz (1 cup or 140 g) brown sugar
3 eggs
4 fl oz (½ cup or 120 ml) sour cream or yogurt
1 teaspoon vanilla
12 oz (2½ cups or 340-350 g) plain flour
2 teaspoons baking powder
4 tablespoons unsweetened cocoa
½ teaspoon ground allspice
l lb (450 g) zucchini, peeled and grated
about 8 oz (1 cup or 225 g) chocolate chips
chopped walnuts (optional)

1. Cream the butter, oil and sugars together until light and fluffy. Then gradually beat in the eggs.
2. Add sour cream and vanilla and mix well.
3. Sift the flour into a bowl and add baking powder, cocoa, and allspice. Gently blend dry ingredients into the creamed mixture.
4. Stir in the grated zucchini and blend well. Add walnuts if desired.
5. Spread batter evenly into a greased 9 x 13 inch (23 x 31 cm) greased baking tin. Sprinkle chocolate chips over the top.
6. Bake for 40-45 minutes in a preheated oven at 350°F (180°C) until the cake is firm and a toothpick inserted in the center comes out clean. Cut into squares while still warm.

Zucchini Bread Loaf

*The addition of grated zucchini will keep the bread fresh longer,
but this loaf is too good to be kept for very long.*

1 lb (450 g) zucchini, coursely grated
1 ¼ lbs (4 cups or 550 g) plain flour
2 teaspoons yeast
4 tablespoons fresh Parmesan cheese, grated
black pepper to taste
2 tablespoons olive oil
water
milk
sesame seeds

1. Grate the zucchini and set aside in a colander to drain for 30 minutes. Pat dry.
2. Mix flour, yeast, Parmesan cheese, and pepper.
3. Add the zucchini and oil. Mix together and add enough lukewarm water to make a firm dough.
4. Knead on a floured board until smooth. Put it back in the mixing bowl, cover, and allow to rise in a warm place until the size has doubled.
5. Remove dough and knead lightly. Then place it in a greased loaf tin. Brush the top with milk and sprinkle with sesame seeds. Allow it to rise again.
6. Bake in a preheated oven at 400°F (200°C) for 25 minutes or until brown and done.

Random Recipes for Rotund Marrows

Marrow Ginger Jam

As marrows become larger, they also become filled with water rather than flavor. Huge marrows are prized by horticultural show judges who do not have to eat them.This is an unusual solution for using up good zucchini that have swelled into bulging marrows, perhaps while you were away on holiday.

4 lbs (2 kg) prepared marrow cubes
3 lbs (1 ½ kg) preserving sugar
1 oz (30 g) root ginger
3 large lemons, thinly peeled rind and juice

1. Prepare marrows by peeling and seeding them, then cutting into cubes.
2. Sprinkle with a third of the sugar and allow to stand overnight.
3. Pound the ginger with a mallet to crush the hard fibrous flesh and to allow flavor to escape.
4. Place ginger and lemon rind in a muslin bag and tie the bag.
5. Put marrow and its juices into a large pot. Add the remaining sugar, the lemon juice and the muslin bag.
6. Cook slowly, making sure sugar is dissolved before the boiling point is reached. Continue to boil steadily until marrow looks transparent. Taste after 15 minutes to adjust flavor, and remove bag if mixture is strong enough. Cook until the setting point is reached.

Stuffed Marrow Rings

Here is a recipe to appreciate when you are 'stuck' with an overgrown, show-size marrow. The Mediterranean rice stuffing will absorb the water and work better than a breadcrumb stuffing which may become soggy.

1 marrow
1 medium onion, chopped
1-2 garlic cloves, chopped
4 fl oz (½ cup or 120 ml) olive oil
8 oz (250 g) rice
1 tablespoon tomato paste (optional)
5 fl oz (150 ml) water
1 tablespoon mint, chopped
1 tablespoon dill weed, chopped
¼ teaspoon ground cinnamon
salt and pepper to taste

1. Cut the large marrow across into rings, about 1 inch (nearly 3 cm) thick. Remove the seeds in the center and blanch the rings for 5 minutes. Arrange the rings in a buttered baking dish.
2. To make the stuffing, heat the oil in a saucepan and sauté the onion and garlic until soft but not browned. Stir in the rice, tomato paste, and water. Simmer for 5 minutes.
3. Add the rest of the ingredients. Remove from heat and season to taste.
4. Fill marrow centers with the stuffing, allowing it to spill over and form a rounded shape.
5. Bake in 375°F (190°C) oven for 45-60 minutes. Serve, allowing one or two rounds per person.

And More Marrows. . . .

Don't forget these recipes for marrows, which have appeared in previous sections.

Marrow Casserole (Casseroles) page 83

Marrow in Tomato Coriander Sauce (Accompaniments) page 139

Spicy Ginger Marrow (Accompaniments) page 140

TABLE OF WEIGHTS AND MEASURES

ZUCCHINI
small zucchini = up to 5-6 oz (140-175 g)
medium zucchini = 6-8 oz (175-225 g)
large zucchini = over 8 oz (225 g)

TEASPOON AND TABLESPOON MEASUREMENTS ARE LEVEL

LIQUID EQUIVALENTS
1 litre = 1000 ml = 1 ¾ Imperial pints = 2 US pints = 4 cups
        600 ml = 1 Imperial pint = 1 ¼ US pint = 2 ½ cups
½ litre = 500 ml = ¾ Imperial pint = 1 US pint = 2 cups
        300 ml = ½ Imperial pint = 1 ¼ cups
¼ litre = 250 ml = 8 fl oz = ½ US pint = 1 cup
        150 ml = 5 fl oz = 2/3 cup
    100-125 ml = 3 ½ - 4 fl oz = 1/3 - ½ cup

WEIGHTS
28 g = 1 oz
110 g = 4 oz or ½ cup
225 g = 8 oz or 1 cup
450 g = 16 oz or 1 lb
1 kg = 2 lbs

SOME INGREDIENT MEASUREMENTS
fresh breadcrumbs   3 ½ oz (100 g) = 2 cups
butter   8 oz (250 g) = 1 cup
cheese, grated   2 oz (50-60 g) = ½ cup
flour   1 lb (500 g) = 3 ¾ cups
                     5 oz (150 g) = 1 cup
sugar   2 oz (50-60 g) = 1/3 cup

COMMENTS ON ZUCCHINI

Courgettes and zucchini are exactly the same thing. The word courgette is a diminutive of the French *courge*, meaning marrow. Zucchini means miniature *zucca*, or gourd, in Italian.

Calabacitas are zucchini in Spain or Mexico.

The zucchini is classified as a summer squash, *cucurbita pepo*, together with marrows and little pattypan squashes.

Zucchini, bushier than other plants in the family, grow over the ground and readily adapt themselves to many soil types.

Zucchini have a long growing season and are satisfying to cultivate as they grow in abundance; the more they are picked, the more they produce. Left uncut, they turn into marrows.

Generally, zucchini have a deep green skin with pale firm flesh, but some varieties are bright yellow, or very light green, or striped.

To cut zucchini from their stems, use a sharp knife and leave about 1 inch (3 cm) of stem with the vegetable.

To prepare zucchini, wash and dry them. Trim the stalk and flower ends. It is not necessary to peel them if they are sufficiently young and tender.

To freeze, prepare zucchini and cut into slices ¼ inch (1 cm) thick. Blanch in boiling water for 1 minute, then plunge them into cold water (to stop them cooking). Pat them dry with paper towels, place them in plastic bags or containers and freeze them. They will keep for up to 6 months.

Grate fresh zucchini when they are plentiful in the garden and store in recipe-size portions in freezer containers.

172

You may achieve an attractive effect by peeling zucchini with a potato peeler, leaving alternate strips of green skin and white flesh.

Zucchini are most loved of all squashes because of their versatility and ease of cooking. They may be steamed or boiled, sautéed in butter, dipped in egg and breadcrumbs and fried, grilled, roasted, or stuffed and baked.

For easy roasting, just place zucchini in an ovenproof dish, sprinkle with crushed garlic, broken basil leaves and olive oil. Then bake in a hot oven until tender, turning slices from time to time.

Grilled zucchini is an ideal vegetable to cook on the outdoor grill over hot coals.

Baby zucchini have no seeds or pith and have flesh that is completely firm. Use small firm zucchini whenever possible, no longer than 6 inches, with a healthy looking shiny skin, as these have more flavor.

Baby zucchini need little or no cooking. Just steam them whole or blanch them. Larger zucchini can be sliced and steamed or boiled with care taken that they are not overcooked and soggy.

Zucchini are usually sliced into rounds. If they are to be stuffed, cut them into half lengthways. Spoon out seeds and flesh without piercing skin and leaving at least ½ inch (1 cm) flesh.

Although zucchini come in a huge range of shapes, sizes, and colors, they have in common their flavor, which is almost exactly the same regardless of appearance.

Marrows are simply overgrown zucchini, but not as firm or as tasteful when cooked.

Vegetable marrow was not introduced to England until the nineteenth century, when it became known, with Mrs. Beeton giving several recipes for it.

Marrows, and all squashes, were a staple food of native American Indians, eaten traditionally with corn and beans. The three vegetables symbolize three inseparable sisters in an Iroquois myth.

Zucchini blossoms, seldom found in shops, may be carefully removed (after waiting for the plants to pollinate) and frozen until enough flowers are collected to cook, perhaps in Zucchini Blossom Soup.

Fragile, rich, yellow zucchini flowers can be dipped in batter and fried to light golden fritters. However, make all the preparations before picking the flowers as they wilt rapidly.

Recent increased demand for the flowers has resulted in the breeding of zucchini plants solely for their flowers with consequent production of tiny baby zucchini.

Zucchini have a high water content—90%.

Zucchini are rich in potassium and Vitamins A (mostly in the skin), C and folic acid. Keep the skin intact as much as possible, as peeling removes nutrients that are just under the skin as well as valuable fiber.

Like eggplants, zucchini absorb fat readily.

Zucchini are available most of the year and will keep for a week stored in the salad compartment of your refrigerator.

Even Agatha Christie's exotic Belgian detective is interested in discovering the mysterious qualities of zucchini. In *The Murder of Roger Ackroyd* (1926), Hercule Poirot has retired to the village of King's Abbot where he plans to cultivate vegetable marrows.